Hands-On Cloud Development with WildFly

Develop, deploy, and configure cloud-based, enterprise Java applications with WildFly Swarm and OpenShift

Tomasz Adamski

BIRMINGHAM - MUMBAI

Hands-On Cloud Development with WildFly

Commissioning Editor: Amarabha Banerjee
Acquisition Editor: Shweta Pant
Content Development Editor: Arun Nadar
Technical Editor: Surabhi Kulkarni
Copy Editor: Dhanya Baburaj
Project Coordinator: Sheejal Shah
Proofreader: Safis Editing
Indexer: Pratik Shirodkar
Graphics: Jason Monteiro
Production Coordinator: Shraddha Falebhai

First published: March 2018

Production reference: 1280318

Published by Packt Publishing Ltd.
Livery Place
35 Livery Street
Birmingham
B3 2PB, UK.

ISBN 978-1-78646-237-4

www.packtpub.com

`mapt.io`

Mapt is an online digital library that gives you full access to over 5,000 books and videos, as well as industry leading tools to help you plan your personal development and advance your career. For more information, please visit our website.

Why subscribe?

- Spend less time learning and more time coding with practical eBooks and Videos from over 4,000 industry professionals

- Improve your learning with Skill Plans built especially for you

- Get a free eBook or video every month

- Mapt is fully searchable

- Copy and paste, print, and bookmark content

PacktPub.com

Did you know that Packt offers eBook versions of every book published, with PDF and ePub files available? You can upgrade to the eBook version at `www.PacktPub.com` and as a print book customer, you are entitled to a discount on the eBook copy. Get in touch with us at `service@packtpub.com` for more details.

At `www.PacktPub.com`, you can also read a collection of free technical articles, sign up for a range of free newsletters, and receive exclusive discounts and offers on Packt books and eBooks.

Contributors

About the author

Tomasz Adamski is a software engineer at RedHat working on WildFly/JBoss EAP application server.

I am grateful to the technical reviewers, Dimitris Andreadis, Stefano Maestri, Bolesław Dawidowicz, and Mateusz Żurowski, for their insightful comments and thought-provoking suggestions. I would also like to thank Shweta Pant, Arun Nadar, Surabhi Kulkarni, and the whole Packt team that worked on the book. Finally, I would like to thank my family for their support during the writing process.

About the reviewers

Deepak Vohra is a consultant and a principal member of the NuBean software company. He is a Sun-certified Java programmer and web component developer and has worked in the fields of XML, Java programming, and Java EE for 10 years. He is the coauthor of *Pro XML Development with Java Technology*; the technical reviewer of *O'Reilly* book WebLogic: *The Definitive Guide*; the technical reviewer for the *Course Technology PTR* book *Ruby Programming* for the Absolute Beginner; and the author of many Packt Publishing books, such as *JDBC 4.0 and Oracle JDeveloper for J2EE Development*.

Filippe Spolti is a software engineer and an open source and cloud computing enthusiast. On a day-to-day basis, he works with middleware products on OpenShift. He was also a technical support engineer who helps customers to solve issues and contributed to open source projects; he contributes to local conferences in Brazil as a speaker and also by coordinating tracks. He holds a bachelor's degree in information system and a specialization in information security and software engineering and has written a book on WildFly and helped other authors by reviewing their books.

> *Sharing knowledge is rewarding, and it also requires dedication and a little time away from family and friends. I am thankful for the support they gave me over the past years.*

Packt is searching for authors like you

If you're interested in becoming an author for Packt, please visit `authors.packtpub.com` and apply today. We have worked with thousands of developers and tech professionals, just like you, to help them share their insight with the global tech community. You can make a general application, apply for a specific hot topic that we are recruiting an author for, or submit your own idea.

Table of Contents

Preface

The mission of the book is to make you familiar with the tools that you can use to develop and deploy Java EE applications in the cloud. You will be led through the whole application development process: creating the application, deploying in the cloud, configuring Continuous Integration, and secure and fault-tolerant communication between the created services. As a result, you will gain practical knowledge of Java EE cloud development, which you can use as a reference for your further projects.

Who this book is for

If you're an experienced developer who's familiar with Java EE technologies and would like to learn how you can use those technologies in the cloud with WildFly and OpenShift, then this book is for you.

What this book covers

Chapter 1, *Java EE and Modern Architectural Methodologies*, gives users an overview of the current state of Java EE and its relevance to modern architectural methodologies, that is, microservices and cloud computing. We will introduce the tools that will be used throughout the book and the application that we will be developing.

Chapter 2, *Getting Familiar with WildFly Swarm*, covers WildFly and how it relates to Java EE and its main features. We will introduce WildFly Swarm—WildFly's side project—describe its purpose, and show how it can be used to develop microservices.

Chapter 3, *Right-Sizing Your Services*, focuses on what Swarm does to create your services with only those dependencies that are necessary for them. You will learn in greater detail what a fraction is, how Swarm detects which fractions should be used, and how you can modify the fraction discovery behavior.

Chapter 4, *Tuning the Configuration of Your Services*, helps you to learn how to configure your Swarm services. We will show you practical examples of different configuration tools that are available and how you can use them to steer the behavior of your applications.

Chapter 5, *Testing Your Services with Arquillian,* teaches you how to test your microservices. This chapter will introduce Arquillian, the testing framework that will be used, and present the purpose of the project and its main features. Later, you will learn how to develop, write, and configure tests for your services based on practical examples.

Chapter 6, *Deploying Applications on the Cloud with OpenShift,* discusses how to deploy those services to the cloud, and this chapter uses OpenShift to achieve that.

Chapter 7, *Configuring Storage for Your Applications,* starts by helping you learn the theoretical basis of OpenShift storage configuration. Later, we will show you how to deploy a database in the cloud and configure your cloud applications to use it.

Chapter 8, *Scaling and Connecting Your Services,* looks in greater detail at the process of deploying, scaling, and connecting your applications running in an OpenShift environment.

Chapter 9, *Configuring Continuous Integration Using Jenkins,* teaches you how to integrate the pet store application with Jenkins, a Continuous Integration server. We will introduce CI concepts and show how they can be implemented using Jenkins.

Chapter 10, *Providing Security Using Keycloak,* deals with the basics of distributed, token-based security. We will introduce Keycloak, an authentication server, that can be used to secure distributed cloud applications. As a practical example, we will secure part of the API of the Petstore application.

Chapter 11, *Adding Resilience Using Hystrix,* discusses how to deal with network failures, which are inevitable in a distributed environment. In order to do that, we will introduce the circuit breaker architectural pattern and cover when it should be used and what are its benefits. We will look at its Netflix implementation, Hystrix. We will cover how it is implemented and how it can be used.

Chapter 12, *Future Direction,* describes briefly what the future of Java EE development is likely to look such as, the plans for evolving the platform and how concepts provided by applications described in the book may be standardized in the future. We will also take a look at MicroProfile and Jakarta EE, describe their purpose, and emphasize how they can help you to move the platform forward at a faster pace.

To get the most out of this book

This book assumes that you are familiar with Java EE technology. Although we will be briefly reminding what Java EE constructs do in the examples, they won't be explained in detail.

The code repository contains the examples from all the chapters. In order to help you navigate through them, the examples are indexed from within the chapters.

Download the example code files

You can download the example code files for this book from your account at `www.packtpub.com`. If you purchased this book elsewhere, you can visit `www.packtpub.com/support` and register to have the files emailed directly to you.

You can download the code files by following these steps:

1. Log in or register at `www.packtpub.com`.
2. Select the **SUPPORT** tab.
3. Click on **Code Downloads & Errata**.
4. Enter the name of the book in the **Search** box and follow the onscreen instructions.

Once the file is downloaded, please make sure that you unzip or extract the folder using the latest version of:

- WinRAR/7-Zip for Windows
- Zipeg/iZip/UnRarX for Mac
- 7-Zip/PeaZip for Linux

The code bundle for the book is also hosted on GitHub at `https://github.com/PacktPublishing/Hands-On-Cloud-Development-with-WildFly`. In case there's an update to the code, it will be updated on the existing GitHub repository.

We also have other code bundles from our rich catalog of books and videos available at `https://github.com/PacktPublishing/`. Check them out!

Download the color images

We also provide a PDF file that has color images of the screenshots/diagrams used in this book. You can download it here:

`https://www.packtpub.com/sites/default/files/downloads/HandsOnCloudDevelopmentwithWildFly_ColorImages.pdf`.

Conventions used

There are a number of text conventions used throughout this book.

`CodeInText`: Indicates code words in text, database table names, folder names, filenames, file extensions, pathnames, dummy URLs, user input, and Twitter handles. Here is an example: "Computer programming books often start with a `Hello World` application."

A block of code is set as follows:

```
package org.packt.swarm;

import javax.ws.rs.GET;
import javax.ws.rs.Path;
import javax.ws.rs.Produces;
```

When we wish to draw your attention to a particular part of a code block, the relevant lines or items are set in bold:

```
package org.packt.swarm;

import javax.ws.rs.ApplicationPath;
import javax.ws.rs.core.Application;

@ApplicationPath("/")
public class HelloWorldApplication extends Application {
}
```

Any command-line input or output is written as follows:

```
mvn wildfly-swarm:run
```

Bold: Indicates a new term, an important word, or words that you see onscreen. For example, words in menus or dialog boxes appear in the text like this. Here is an example: "we have to click on the **Create a route** in **Services** menu of the web console."

Warnings or important notes appear like this.

Tips and tricks appear like this.

Get in touch

Feedback from our readers is always welcome.

General feedback: Email `feedback@packtpub.com` and mention the book title in the subject of your message. If you have questions about any aspect of this book, please email us at `questions@packtpub.com`.

Errata: Although we have taken every care to ensure the accuracy of our content, mistakes do happen. If you have found a mistake in this book, we would be grateful if you would report this to us. Please visit `www.packtpub.com/submit-errata`, selecting your book, clicking on the Errata Submission Form link, and entering the details.

Piracy: If you come across any illegal copies of our works in any form on the Internet, we would be grateful if you would provide us with the location address or website name. Please contact us at `copyright@packtpub.com` with a link to the material.

If you are interested in becoming an author: If there is a topic that you have expertise in and you are interested in either writing or contributing to a book, please visit `authors.packtpub.com`.

Reviews

Please leave a review. Once you have read and used this book, why not leave a review on the site that you purchased it from? Potential readers can then see and use your unbiased opinion to make purchase decisions, we at Packt can understand what you think about our products, and our authors can see your feedback on their book. Thank you!

For more information about Packt, please visit `packtpub.com`.

Java EE and Modern Architectural Methodologies

In this chapter, we will give users an overview of the current state of **Java Enterprise Edition** (**EE**) and its relevance in modern architectural methodologies, that is, **microservices** and **cloud computing**. We will introduce the tools that will be used throughout the book and the application that we will be developing.

Let's start by recalling a few basic facts about Java EE.

Java EE

Before sketching the Java EE architecture, let's take a quick look at the process through which the standard is created.

Java Community Process

Java EE is a standard designed for building enterprise applications with the Java programming language. It contains a number of specifications, which define functionalities required by implementations of the standard.

Specifications that constitute Java EE are developed in an open, community-based process. Both organizations and individual users can join it and take part in the development.

As a standard, Java EE may possess multiple implementations. A vendor who is willing to create a product that is Java EE-certified has to pass a technology compliance test, which guarantees that the product is in alignment with the standard.

The standard provides the contract between enterprise application developers and the vendors of standard implementations. An application developer can be sure that their application will be supported and portable, as there are a number of standard implementations; they are not dependent on one vendor. Application developers are free to migrate their applications between different standard implementations.

It is also important to note that the standard does not determine the details of server implementation. As a result, vendors have to compete to provide the most efficient, robust, and easy-to-use implementation.

To sum up, the Java EE standard provides enterprise application developers with an ability to write supported and portable applications. Furthermore, the community-based specification development process and competition between vendors help the standard to evolve and allows users to choose the best implementation for their needs.

On the flip side, the fact that Java EE is a standard implementation result in a slower evolution and decision-making process than alternative frameworks. In a world in which technology is being developed rapidly, this becomes a bigger problem. As a result, recently, an effort has been made to refactor the way in which standards and specifications are created. Java EE is currently transforming into EE4J, a standard developed under Eclipse Foundation's governance. We will return to this topic in the final `Chapter 12`: *Future Directions*.

The basic architecture of Java EE applications

Java EE applications are written in the Java language and run on **Java virtual machine (JVM)**. On top of the standard Java SE functionality, the Java EE implementation provider implements a number of services, which can be used by those applications. Examples of such services may be security, transactions, or dependency injection.

Applications don't interact with enterprise services directly. Instead, the specifications define the **component** and **containers** concepts. Components are software units written in the Java language and configured and built in a similar way to standard Java classes. The difference is that metatada provided with the component allows it to be run using a runtime provided by the Java EE implementation. Such a runtime, which may differ for the different types of component, is called a container. The container is responsible for providing access to all enterprise services required by the component.

As an example, let's take a look at the following component:

```java
package org.tadamski.examples.javaee;

import org.tadamski.examples.java.ee.model.Foo;

import javax.ejb.Stateless;
import javax.enterprise.event.Event;
import javax.inject.Inject;
import javax.persistence.EntityManager;

//1
@Stateless
public class FooDaoBean implements FooDao {

    //2
    @Inject
    private EntityManager em;


    public void save(Foo foo) throws Exception {
        //3
        em.persist(foo);
    }
}
```

The preceding script presents an `ejb` component (1), that is, `FooDaoBean`, which is responsible for saving objects of the `Foo` type into the database.

The `ejb` container in which this component will run will be responsible for pooling instances of this component and managing the lifecycle for all of them. Furthermore, this concrete component takes advantage of the number of enterprise services: dependency injection (2), ORM persistence (3), and transactions (the default for this kind of component).

In general, the goal of the Java EE runtime is to take care of all technical aspects of enterprise applications so that the application developer can concentrate on writing business code. The preceding example demonstrates how it is realized in Java EE: the application developer writes their code using POJOs with minimal configuration (provided mostly by annotations). The code written by an application developer implements business functionalities declaratively, informing middleware about its technical requirements.

The scope of the Java EE standard

Traditionally, business applications written in the Java EE technology were based on a three-tier architectures, web, business, and enterprise information system tier:

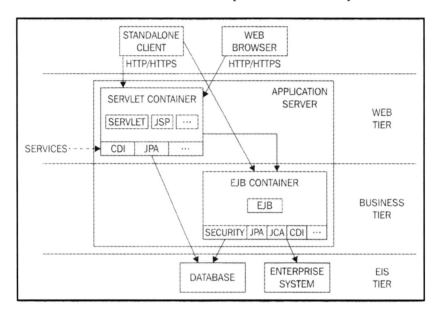

Application server implements web and business tiers. It can be accessed by various types of clients

Web components, such as **Servlets**, JSPs, or JAX-RS, allow for the implementation of the web layer. They are able to respond to the HTTP requests from different kinds of clients. For example, JSF may be used to create web user interfaces in a convenient way, whereas the JAX-RS API allows for the implementation of RESTful services.

The business layer is implemented by EJBs, pooled POJO-based components that allow for the easy implementation of transactional operations and that can provide a wide array of capabilities such as security, database, external system integration, remote access, or dependency injection.

Although the bird's-eye view architecture is quite straightforward, it is very elastic and allows for the implementation of a wide array of enterprise applications. Moreover, the standard has evolved throughout the years, providing tools for a wide array enterprise usage.

If you take a look at Java EE specification (Further Reading, link 1) you will be able to see all the specifications that are part of the standard. The shared amount of them may be intimidating at first slight. It should be noted that, in most cases, you will have to deal with only a subset of those. On the other hand, when your applications require any kind of enterprise functionality, it is highly probable that the needed tool is already there for you—integrated with the whole platform and easy to use.

Implementation of Java EE standard

Java EE standard implementations are runtimes that allow us to run the components and provide them with the services specified in the Java EE standard. Such runtimes are called **application servers**.

Application developers create components based on the specification. Those components are assembled into archives, which can be deployed on application servers.

Application servers allow for the deployment of a number of applications. Furthermore, as hinted at the beginning of this chapter, an application can change the server implementation and deploy archives using the application server from the other vendor:

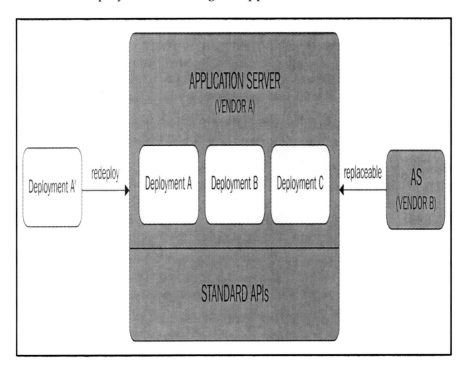

Current development trends

The way applications are developed evolves over time. Let's sketch concepts that have had a big impact on software development in recent years: cloud computing and microservices.

Cloud computing

Cloud computing is an infrastructure that makes it possible to automatically provision computing resources on demand. The types of resource provided depend on the contract between the cloud provider and the customer—the cloud provider can provide software services, such as email or disk storage, platforms for software development, access to virtual machines, or infrastructure for running software applications.

The resources are provided dynamically and rapidly using the internet, and, as a result, the customer is able to use (and pay) for resources that they currently use. The cloud provider, on the other hand, can take advantage of economies of scale: specialization and optimal resource usage will result in quality improvements and cost optimization.

So, how does interaction with cloud computing infrastructures look from the developer's point of view? During the development, the cloud provider provides a platform that contains a number of tools: it enables developers to run multiple application frameworks, standalone services, and databases among others. It provides functionalities and tools needed by those applications: scaling, networking, security, and communication. Furthermore, as hinted earlier, a user pays only for the resources used; cloud infrastructure will adjust the resources provided based on the load used by your application.

The preceding description sounds promising, but it immediately raises a number of questions, such as how are the resources provisioned and scaled, what kinds of tools can I use, and what are the APIs for the tools provided.

One of the goals of this book is to provide you with all this information throughout. For the purpose of this introductory chapter, it is enough to acknowledge the most important information: cloud computing infrastructures will enable us to develop and deploy with a wide array of tools using computing resources provided on demand.

Microservices

Microservices architecture is a software development methodology that advocates creating an application from loosely coupled services that cooperate together.

Such an architecture was researched and advertised for a long period of time: Some time ago, a lot of attention was given to **Service-Oriented Architecture** (**SOA**). Even earlier, **CORBA**, the standard for distributed computing, was designed. Furthermore, building your applications with loosely coupled, highly cohesive services is a good software practice, and it can (and should) also be applied in a traditional monolithic application. Why has the new concept been created then, and what distinguishes it?

In recent years, a number of companies building large distributed systems have found it harder to build and maintain their systems using the traditional monolithic software architectures and decided to refactor their systems to loosely coupled modular distributed systems. Looking at the experience of those companies that succeeded in doing so, we were able to gather common architectural patterns in the systems that they built. This gave birth to the microservice architecture concept. Put in another way, microservices can be thought of as a software architecture that is another iteration of distributed computing systems, whose characteristics were derived from practical experience. As a result, instead of providing a definition of microservice architectures to which all aspiring implementors have to adhere, it is easier to provide a common set of characteristics that microservice systems share (Further Reading, link 2). Let's do it now.

Microservices are built as standalone services that are independently deployable. From the technical point of view, it means that they run in different processes and communicate through the network using their APIs. Each of the services can be started, stopped, and updated independently. Each service is responsible for its own data and can modify the data of other services using only their API.

The system is decomposed into microservices around business functionalities. Each microservices is built by one, small team that consists of all necessary technical specialists. For example, in a store application, there may be a review service. The review service team may consist of programmers, database engineers, testers, and domain experts. The team is responsible for every aspect of this service—from getting customer feedback to database administration.

As you can see, instead of advertising a set of recommended characteristics that the applications should adhere to, successful microservice practitioners have created a technological environment that enforces modularity and loose coupling.

So, if you successfully implement a microservice architecture, what benefits will you obtain?

Advantages of implementing microservices

The first thing that is straightforward but should be emphasized is that if you successfully create a system whose architectural characteristics-force modularity and loose coupling, you will obtain a highly modular system as ad hoc fixes and extensions won't compromise and effectively abandon the boundaries between services throughout the development process.

Because of the modular characteristics of developed applications, components that constitute them may be developed more effectively: As there is a small, cross-sectional team working on each service, its members can concentrate on their own area of work relatively independently of other teams. As the practice suggests, as the team grows communication starts to inhibit work more and more. The small, focused team knows the domain well, and they also know each other well, can communicate immediately, and move the work forward.

Also, crucial is the fact that the service can be deployed independently of other services. A successful microservices architecture does not have the concept of big system release in which all teams gather their recent updates together and create a major release of the whole system. Instead, all teams are able to release and deploy their new functionalities independently of other services. There is no synchronization between the teams, and if there is a new version of a service that can be released, the service's team can just independently design to do it. Such a characteristic is a catalyst for Continous Integration. The team is able to build the pipeline so that each code triggers a test, review, and deploy process.

The characteristics described in the preceding paragraph—small, focused teams and independent and automated build and deployment processess—lead to very important characteristics of the successful microservices-based system: an ability to implement required changes very fast. This is crucial, as it allows for immediate responses to customer needs. This tightens the feedback loop between the customer and developer and allows the system to quickly evolve to meet the customer needs.

Last but not least, we should mention the direct technical consequences. Microservices can be scaled more effectively: When scaling a traditional monolith application, we need to replicate a number of application servers effectively, replicating all the functionalities implemented in the application. Scaling microservices can be more fine-grained; we are able to replicate only the services that need more instances across different servers.

Furthermore, microservices architecture tends to improve the availability: if a review service is down, the rest of the store can work regardless of it. Such a situation is obviously far from ideal but way better than a shutdown of the whole system.

In the preceding paragraph, we mentioned that the preceding characteristics apply to successful microservices implementation. As it turns out, creating such systems is not simple. Let's learn why.

Challenges of implementing microservices

The challenges that encompass implementing microservice architecture can be summarized in one phrase: distributed system.

Is the functionality that you will implement will use a bunch of services throughout a network. You will have to deal with network delays and failures. What if the response is not immediate? Is the target service down or busy? How should we find out, and what we should do about it?

Should the data belong to one microservice? Easier said than done. We can make the database underlying the service consistent, but how do we propagate this information to other services that rely on this data?

Also, it is nice that each team can work independently, but what if we really need to implement cross-service functionality? That can become a pain: a cross-team endeavor that may introduce large architectural changes and substantially impact the whole architecture.

Let's assume that we managed to deal with the preceding problems and have a running system. What happens when an error occurs? We will have to analyze logs scattered around a number of services, also tracing network interactions between all of them.

So, how should you decide whether the microservice architecture is suitable for your application?

When to adopt the microservice architecture

Microservices should primarily be considered for systems in which managing the traditional monolithic application has become too complex to develop and maintain. If you are developing a small application, additional complexity, described in the preceding paragraph, may outweigh the modularity benefits and inhibit, instead of amplifying, your development process.

It has been suggested (*Further Reading*, link 3) that microservices architecture should be an evolution of the monolith application. Most systems should start as a monolith, and the transition to microservices should only be considered when the system grows to the extent that it becomes too hard to develop and maintain.

Last but not least, if the system is badly designed, the transition to microservices won't magically solve its problems. To put it more bluntly, distributing a messy system will result in an even greater mess. As we have already mentioned, microservices should be considered as a solution when the complexity of the system requires imposing modularity and not as a magical fix for badly written software.

Microservices and the cloud

In order to implement a successful microservices architecture, we will need to automate as much of the infrastructure as possible. Eventually, we will be dealing with a system containing a large number of independent services running somewhere across the network. Maintaining such systems manually is virtually impossible.

We will like each service to be automatically built, tested, scaled, and monitored. The cloud infrastructure is a natural microservices environment, which allows you to achieve that. Each service can be run and scaled on resources provided on demand, and the tools available will allow us to build, test, and connect the services in a fault-tolerant way.

You will learn about all of those in this book.

It's time to look how Java EE can fit into the cloud-microservices picture.

Java EE microservices

As mentioned in *The basic architecture of Java EE applications* section, traditionally, in Java EE, you were creating JARs with your applications and deploying them on an application server. With microservices, we will like to transform the same kind of JARs into runnable services:

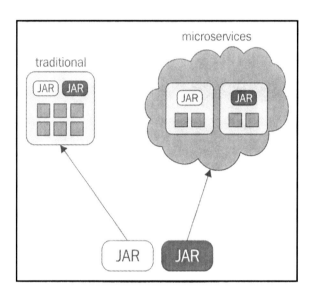

In a traditional scenario, the application server has to support all the APIs specified in the standard.

In a microservices scenario, we will like to transform each JAR, which is an implementation of a microservice, into a runnable JAR. This can be done by creating a runtime for the given microservice and assembling this runtime and the service's archive into a runnable JAR. Since the assembled runtime will be used by only one service, we don't have to include all the Java EE modules in it. The tool that builds your microservices will have to analyze your service's archive and create a runtime, which contains only those functionalities that are required by it.

We have already sketched how we can use Java EE as a base for microservices architecture, but what are the benefits that you will achieve by doing so? Firstly, you will be able to take advantage of proven technologies and your experience with them immediately. Moreover, there is a portability aspect. As we covered in the preceding section, you are encouraged to start with monolithic applications and refactor it microservices, if necessary. Owing to the common set of technologies used and the standard archive format that is used in both scenarios, you can easily migrate between the two, creating an elastic architecture that can be changed and refactored when necessary.

The goal of the book

As you are going to learn in this book, you are able to use your existing Java EE knowledge to create microservices architecture. This knowledge will not be sufficient though, because, as we mentioned in the *Microservices* section, this kind of architecture introduces its own complexity, which has to be handled.

The goal of this book is to fill this knowledge gap by providing you with a practical, hands-on introduction to the development of microservice-based applications running on cloud infrastructures. This book makes an assumption that you are familiar with Java EE and the traditional way of developing Java EE applications. It will complement this knowledge with the information about a concrete set of tools that will allow you to immediately take advantage of both cloud computing and microservices.

We will like to emphasize that this book does not advertise any particular methodology, and, as we mentioned in the *Microservices* section, any architecture decision should be made with regard to the concrete project, taking into consideration all the advantages and disadvantages. Our goal is to provide you with a set of tools so that if you decide to make such a transition, you will immediately know what to do.

Throughout the book, we will develop a sample application, which will serve as a base for all our examples. Let's learn more about it now.

The pet store application

Computer programming books often start with the `Hello World` application. Similarly, books describing a framework often develop a pet store application. We will follow this tradition. The pet store that we will develop will be a simple application that will allow you to browse the catalog of pets, add some of them to your cart, and finalize the payment.

During the development of the application, we will be concentrating on cloud and microservice aspects. The service code is simple and uses basic Java EE technologies so that the reader can concentrate on what is being taught in this book: cloud integration and microservices development.

Let's take the bird's-eye view of the application:

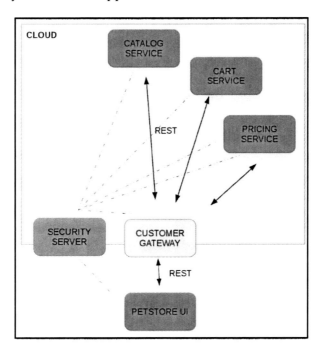

The backend services (red), gateways (yellow), and security server (blue) are deployed in a cloud. The UI application (green) is deployed outside the cloud.

The gateway services are responsible for providing APIs for different users. The customer gateway provides an API for customers, which is used by petstore-ui—web-client implementing the store interface. The customer gateway orchestrates invocations to the underlying base services and is accessible from outside the cloud.

The security service is responsible for the authentication and authorization of access to different parts of the API. It is used by all other components. The security service is accessible from outside the cloud.

The core functionalities are implemented by backend services. Backend services are not accessible from the gateway service. Let's take a look at their functions:

- Catalog service: Provides information about pets available in the store
- Pricing service: Responsible for providing the price of a given pet
- Cart service: Responsible for keeping information about the cart of a given customer

We will develop the application step by step throughout the book. The application is attached to the book, and as a result, you could work with it immediately while learning various concepts described in the book.

The technologies used

We will convert our traditional Java EE JARs into runnable ones using WildFly Swarm—the tool that we will introduce in Chapter 2, *Get Familiar with WildFly Swarm*. WildFly Swarm is able to wrap our application into a JAR containing a minimal number of libraries needed for it, effectively creating microservices from a deployable JAR. We will cover how Swarm does it in Chapter 3, *Right-Size Your Applications*, and how to configure the created services in Chapter 4, *Tuning the Configuration of Your Services*.

After services are written, we have to write tests for them. We will use the Arquillian library to do it. We will discuss how to use it in Chapter 5, *Testing Your Services with Arquillian*.

We will deploy the created services in cloud using OpenShift. In Chapter 6, *Deploying Applications on the Cloud with OpenShift*, we will give you a theoretical introduction to the platform, the API, and tools that it provides. In Chapter 7, *Configuring Persistent Storage for your Applications*, we will discuss how to configure persistent storage for our applications on OpenShift and how to scale and connect our services.

Creating and deploying applications in cloud is not enough for them to be ready for production. We still need to secure them, monitor them, and take care of network failures.

To provide security, we will take advantage of the Keycloak server. In order to take care of network failures, we will use the Hystrix library. In order to provide monitoring.

Summary

This chapter was intended to give you an overview of what you can expect from reading this book.

We have recalled basic information about Java EE and the traditional way in which it was used to develop enterprise application. Later, we introduced modern trends in software development: cloud computing and microservices architecture.

Then, we introduced the pet store—the sample application that we are going to develop throughout the book.

Finally, we introduced all the technologies and tools used throughout the book, such as WildFly Swarm, OpenShift, Hystrix, Jenkins, and Keycloak.

Further reading

1. http://www.oracle.com/technetwork/java/javaee/overview/index.html
2. https://www.youtube.com/watch?v=wgdBVIX9ifA
3. https://martinfowler.com/bliki/MonolithFirst.html

Getting Familiar with WildFly Swarm 2

In this chapter, we will cover WildFly—how it relates to Java EE and its main features. We will introduce WildFly Swarm—WildFly's child project—describe its purpose, and show how it can be used to develop microservices. We will create and deploy our first application using Swarm.

Introducing WildFly

Most of you have probably heard about JBoss Application Server; WildFly is its successor. It is an open source implementation of the Java EE specification, and, more importantly in the context of this book, it is the base of Swarm project.

WildFly has an extensible architecture, which enables building differently sized distributions on top of its high-performance core, which, as we will learn in the next chapter, is utilized by Swarm to a great extent.

Performance

When you hear the phrase *Java EE application server,* the first thing that may come to your mind is the word *heavyweight,* as this is the way in which application servers are often described. It's worth noting however that the Java EE specification doesn't prescribe for its implementation to be slow and bloated, and many modern application servers (WildFly included) indeed don't follow that nonexistent rule.

WildFly starts within seconds and is highly optimized in terms of resource usage. You are going to see it many times throughout the book. We are going to run a number of WildFly based services and tests, all of them running immediately and with small memory footprint.

Extensible nature

As mentioned earlier, WildFly's default distribution is a Java EE application server with all necessary libraries. Owing to the extensible nature of WildFly, you can easily create your own server distribution. It is possible to trim unused subsystems; a good example here may be the web profile, which contains only those subsystems that are needed to serve web pages and may be treated as a web server. It is also easy to add your own extensions to provide additional functions.

As you will learn later in this book, Swarm takes advantage of a great detail from both of these abilities, automatically trimming the server so that it uses only the libraries needed by your service, and also provides a bunch of microservices-dedicated extensions.

 Whatever distribution you are going to use, whether it is a trimmed-down web server, a full distribution extended with your own subsystems, or Swarm microservices, it can take advantage of all the features provided by the core, such as high performance, modular classloading, and a mature management layer.

Deployment model

Application servers provide enterprise functionality collocated in a JVM, which can be used by multitenant applications. Those applications can share services, be deployed and undeployed in real time, and communicate with each other in a JVM.

In this book, we will concentrate on Swarm-based microservices, but note that this is a valid architecture model with benefits that should be taken into consideration when choosing the right architectural style for the problems that you are solving.

Components of a monolithic application are located in the same JVM, and they can communicate directly within its boundaries. In such an application, you don't have to think about a number of problems inherent to distributed systems. If you decide to distribute your application, you will have to take care of network failures, service discovery, monitoring service availability, and dealing with their failures, just to name a few problems. Also, in a monolithic application, you can use out-of-the-box technologies, such as transactions or security, that have been thoroughly tested and have proven to work well.

Meet WildFly Swarm

As we discussed earlier, the application server provides the possibility to deploy and manage multiple applications within the same instance. Also, the Java EE-compliant application server provides an implementation of all specifications gathered around Java EE umbrella so that each application that conforms to it can use it.

Such a functionality is not necessary for all application architectures. In services developed in our example application, we might not care much about management, hot redeployment, and support for all Java EE libraries. The reason for that is that we will be developing small focused microservices. If a microservice is updated, we can just kill its container and restart its new version. Also, at the time of service creation, we will be able to determine all the libraries that it will use during its operations. Because of that, we will be able to build the executable JAR with only those necessary dependencies, minimizing the runtime size and memory usage. The tool that is most suitable for such a purpose is WildFly Swarm.

WildFly Swarm is a child project of WildFly, whose goal is to make microservice application development easy. Before we take a deeper look at Swarm behavior, let's get a feel for it using our first `Hello World` JAX-RS Swarm service.

Java EE application

Let's create a simple Java EE application with a REST resource, which uses the `GET` method to serve the `Hello world!` message:

```
package org.packt.swarm;

import javax.ws.rs.GET;
import javax.ws.rs.Path;
import javax.ws.rs.Produces;

//1
```

```
@Path("/")
public class HelloWorldResource {

    //2
    @GET
    //3
    @Path("hello")
    @Produces({ "text/plain" })
      public String hello() {
        return "Hello World!";
    }
}
```

In the listing above, we create a simple resource taking advantage of JAX-RS annotations; we define the main path for the whole class (1) and create the "hello" method, which is annotated with GET(2) and Path(3) annotations so that the "hello" method is executed when the HTML get method is invoked on a "/hello" path.

Furthermore, we have to define the application on the Path (1) root to bootstrap the web application:

```
package org.packt.swarm;

import javax.ws.rs.ApplicationPath;
import javax.ws.rs.core.Application;

//1
@ApplicationPath("/")
public class HelloWorldApplication extends Application {
}
```

Finally, we have to configure pom.xml:

```
<?xml version="1.0" encoding="UTF-8"?>
<project xmlns="http://maven.apache.org/POM/4.0.0"
        xmlns:xsi="http://www.w3.org/2001/XMLSchema-instance"
        xsi:schemaLocation="http://maven.apache.org/POM/4.0.0
http://maven.apache.org/xsd/maven-4.0.0.xsd">
    <modelVersion>4.0.0</modelVersion>

    <!-- 1 -->
    <groupId>org.packt.swarm</groupId>
    <artifactId>swarm-hello-world</artifactId>
    <version>1.0</version>
    <packaging>war</packaging>

    (...)
```

```xml
<!-- 2 -->
<dependencyManagement>
    <dependencies>
        <dependency>
            <groupId>org.jboss.spec</groupId>
            <artifactId>jboss-javaee-7.0</artifactId>
            <version>${version.jboss.spec.javaee.7.0}</version>
            <type>pom</type>
            <scope>import</scope>
        </dependency>
    </dependencies>
</dependencyManagement>

<!-- 3 -->
<dependencies>
    <dependency>
        <groupId>org.jboss.spec.javax.ws.rs</groupId>
        <artifactId>jboss-jaxrs-api_2.0_spec</artifactId>
        <scope>provided</scope>
    </dependency>
</dependencies>

<build>
    <!-- 4 -->
    <plugins>
        <plugin>
            <artifactId>maven-war-plugin</artifactId>
            <version>${version.war.plugin}</version>
            <configuration>
                <failOnMissingWebXml>false</failOnMissingWebXml>
            </configuration>
        </plugin>
    </plugins>
</build>

</project>
```

We are creating the application with the war type (1) so that it can be used as a web application. We are referencing the Java EE (2) and jaxrs API (3) so that we are able to use annotations mentioned in the preceding paragraph. Finally, we have to tweak the war plugin to inform it that we will not use the web.xml file.

That's it. This is the simple REST HelloWorld resource. We will now be able to build it and deploy it on a Java EE application server.

Adapting to WildFly Swarm

Now we all know how to create Java EE applications, described previously, but we are here to learn how to use WildFly Swarm, so let's adopt the preceding application for it. Let's roll up our sleeves as we have some hard work to do now.

We have to modify `pom.xml`:

```
(...)

    <dependencies>
        <!-- 1 -->
        <dependency>
            <groupId>org.wildfly.swarm</groupId>
            <artifactId>jaxrs</artifactId>
            <version>${version.wildfly.swarm}</version>
        </dependency>
    </dependencies>

    <build>
        <plugins>
            (...)
            <!-- 2 -->
            <plugin>
                <groupId>org.wildfly.swarm</groupId>
                <artifactId>wildfly-swarm-plugin</artifactId>
                <version>${version.wildfly.swarm}</version>
                <executions>
                    <execution>
                        <goals>
                            <goal>package</goal>
                        </goals>
                    </execution>
                </executions>
            </plugin>
        </plugins>
    </build>

</project>
```

We had to add dependencies to Swarm's JAX-RS module (1). Such modules are called fractions and you will learn more about them in the next chapter. Please note that we don't need to configure the JAX-RS API dependency directly as it will be provided as the JAX-RS fraction dependency.

Later, we had to configure WildFly Swarm's Maven plugin, which is responsible for building Swarm microservices (2). You will also learn more about it in the next chapter.

That's it. Congratulations! You have just created your first WildFly Swarm application.

 Examples reference: `chapter2/swarm-hello-world` (the whole example is available in the attached code, in the directory: `chapter2/swarm-hello-world` directory.)

Does it really work?

Before we look in greater detail at what happened, let's run the application to prove that it is indeed working. Open the console, enter the root directory of the application, and run the following command:

```
mvn wildfly-swarm:run
```

The Maven command runs successfully:

```
[org.jboss.as.security] (ServerService Thread Pool -- 18) WFLYSEC0002: Activating Secu
[org.jboss.as.security] (MSC service thread 1-3) WFLYSEC0001: Current PicketBox versic
[org.xnio.nio] (ServerService Thread Pool -- 17) XNIO NIO Implementation Version 3.5.4
[org.wildfly.extension.io] (ServerService Thread Pool -- 17) WFLYIO001: Worker 'defaul
[org.wildfly.extension.undertow] (MSC service thread 1-8) WFLYUT0003: Undertow 1.4.18.
[org.wildfly.extension.undertow] (MSC service thread 1-5) WFLYUT0012: Started server d
[org.wildfly.extension.undertow] (MSC service thread 1-5) WFLYUT0006: Undertow HTTP li
[org.jboss.as.server] (Controller Boot Thread) WFLYSRV0212: Resuming server
[org.jboss.as] (Controller Boot Thread) WFLYSRV0025: WildFly Swarm 2018.3.0 (WildFly C
[org.wildfly.swarm.runtime.deployer] (main) deploying swarm-hello-world-1.0.war
[org.jboss.as.server.deployment] (MSC service thread 1-2) WFLYSRV0027: Starting deploy
[org.wildfly.extension.undertow] (MSC service thread 1-1) WFLYUT0018: Host default-hos
[org.jboss.resteasy.resteasy_jaxrs.i18n] (ServerService Thread Pool -- 10) RESTEASY002
[org.wildfly.extension.undertow] (ServerService Thread Pool -- 10) WFLYUT0021: Registe
[org.jboss.as.server] (mai... WFLYSRV0010: Deployed "swarm-hell... rld-1.0.war" (runtim
[org.wildfly.swarm] (main) WFSWARM99999: WildFly Swarm is Ready
```

swarm-hello-world example's console output

We can open the web browser and enter the address of our application, as shown in the following screenshot:

What has just happened here?

The application works indeed. Let's look step by step what has just happened:

1. Maven build has been run. A standard maven package plugin has created the war archive, which included classes described previously (and which can be as well deployed into the standard application server).
2. The Swarm plugin built a runtime for our application. The runtime is based on WildFly-core and contains only the libraries needed by the service application.
3. The plugin has built a runnable JAR, which combines the runtime and the application.
4. Since we have specified the run goal, the plugin has started the service immediately after its creation.

Let's take a look at the target directory to note the build output:

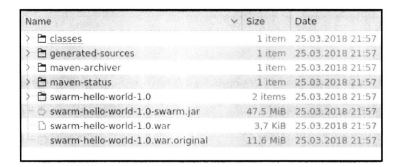

As you can see in the preceding screenshot, besides the standard Maven target artifact, one more JAR is created: **swarm-hello-world-1.0-swarm.jar**. This is the runnable microservice. Its name is created from the archive's name to which the Swarm suffix is added. Also, note that the size of the service is 47,5 MB. It is slightly bigger than WildFly web-server profile. The reason for that is that some more libraries (enabling REST services) have to be added to the server.

This example was supposed to give you an initial feel for WildFly Swarm. As you see, the responsibility of the developer here is to implement a business functionality and configure the Swarm maven plugin. Swarm takes care of the rest: it creates the server with all libraries necessary to make those features work and connects the archive with this server to create a runnable microservice. Owing to this convention-over-configuration style and automatic server creation, a lot of the configuration burden is taken away from the developer so he/she can concentrate on business functionality development. Obviously, this standard behavior can be changed—you will learn more about it in subsequent parts of this book.

Summary

The goal of this chapter was to introduce you to WildFly Swarm—to put it in the context of WildFly, its parent project, show its architecture, features, and benefits. Finally, to give you your first taste of WildFly Swarm, we created a simple web application and used Swarm to create a microservice from it. In the next chapter, we will learn more about the modular nature of WildFly Swarm.

Further reading

1. `http://wildfly.org/`
2. `http://wildfly-swarm.io/`

Right-Sizing Your Services 3

In this chapter, you will learn what Swarm does to create your services with only those dependencies that are necessary for them. You will learn in greater detail what a fraction is, how Swarm detects what fractions should be used, and how you can modify the fraction discovery behavior. Finally, you will learn how to further modify the service creation size and behavior using hollow JARs and thin JARs.

Before we explain all of that, we will introduce the service on which we are going to work.

Catalog service

In the first chapter, you learned the basic architecture of the pet store sample application and the services that constitute it. In this and the next chapter, we will be working with the catalog service. To recall, this is the service responsible for providing the information about pets available in the store. We are going to introduce that simple functionality now. In the next three chapters, we will modify that code in order to show you different features and configuration options of WildFly Swarm. Let's look at the initial version.

Draft version

We will start by introducing the first, draft version of the service, which we will examine and extend later.

Examples reference: `chapter3/catalog-service-jaxrs`.

As in the preceding chapter, we have to start with the `pom.xml`:

```xml
<?xml version="1.0" encoding="UTF-8"?>
<project xmlns="http://maven.apache.org/POM/4.0.0"
        xmlns:xsi="http://www.w3.org/2001/XMLSchema-instance"
        xsi:schemaLocation="http://maven.apache.org/POM/4.0.0
http://maven.apache.org/xsd/maven-4.0.0.xsd">
    <modelVersion>4.0.0</modelVersion>

    <groupId>org.packt.swarm.petstore</groupId>
    <artifactId>catalog-service-jaxrs</artifactId>
    <version>1.0</version>
    <packaging>war</packaging>

    (...)
    <dependencies>
        <!-- 1 -->
        <dependency>
            <groupId>org.wildfly.swarm</groupId>
            <artifactId>jaxrs</artifactId>
            <version>${version.wildfly.swarm}</version>
        </dependency>
    </dependencies>

    <build>
        <plugins>
            <plugin>
                <artifactId>maven-war-plugin</artifactId>
                <version>${version.war.plugin}</version>
                <configuration>
                    <failOnMissingWebXml>false</failOnMissingWebXml>
                </configuration>
            </plugin>
            <!-- 2 -->
            <plugin>
                <groupId>org.wildfly.swarm</groupId>
                <artifactId>wildfly-swarm-plugin</artifactId>
                <version>${version.wildfly.swarm}</version>
                <executions>
                    <execution>
                        <goals>
                            <goal>package</goal>
                        </goals>
                    </execution>
                </executions>
            </plugin>
        </plugins>
```

```
    </build>

</project>
```

We have to add the dependency to JAX-RS fraction (1) and configure the WildFly Swarm plugin (2). Let's move to the code now.

We will start with a simple domain class, Item, which contains information about the pets available in the store:

```java
package org.packt.swarm.petstore.catalog.model;

public class Item {


    private String itemId;
    private String name;
    private int quantity;

    private String description;

    public String getItemId() {
        return itemId;
    }

    public void setItemId(String itemId) {
        this.itemId = itemId;
    }

    public String getName() {
        return name;
    }

    public void setName(String name) {
        this.name = name;
    }

    public int getQuantity() {
        return quantity;
    }

    public void setQuantity(int quantity) {
        this.quantity = quantity;
    }

    public String getDescription() {
        return description;
```

```
    }

    public void setDescription(String description) {
        this.description = description;
    }
}
```

As you can see in the preceding code, this is a simple class containing `itemId`, `name`, description of the pet, and the quantity available in the store. As in the `Hello World` example, we have to initialize our JAX-RS application:

```
package org.packt.swarm.petstore.catalog;

import javax.ws.rs.ApplicationPath;
import javax.ws.rs.core.Application;

@ApplicationPath("/")
public class CatalogApplication extends Application {
}
```

Finally, we are ready to write a simple JAX-RS resource that will serve up information about available pets from the in-memory `HashMap`:

```
package org.packt.swarm.petstore.catalog;

import org.packt.swarm.petstore.catalog.model.Item;

import javax.ws.rs.GET;
import javax.ws.rs.Path;
import javax.ws.rs.PathParam;
import javax.ws.rs.Produces;
import javax.ws.rs.core.MediaType;
import javax.ws.rs.core.Response;
import java.util.HashMap;
import java.util.Map;

//1
@Path("/")
public class CatalogResource {

    //2
    private Map<String, Item> catalog = new HashMap<>();

    public CatalogResource(){
        Item turtle = new Item();
        turtle.setItemId("turtle");
        turtle.setName("turtle");
```

```
        turtle.setQuantity(5);
        turtle.setDescription("Slow, friendly reptile. Let your busy self
see how it spends 100 years of his life laying on sand and swimming.");
        catalog.put("turtle", turtle);
    }

    //3
    @GET
    @Path("item/{itemId}")
    @Produces(MediaType.APPLICATION_JSON)
    public Response searchById(@PathParam("itemId") String itemId) {
        try {
            Item item = catalog.get(itemId);
            return Response.ok(item).build();
        } catch (Exception e) {
            return
Response.status(Response.Status.BAD_REQUEST).entity(e.getMessage()).build()
;
        }
    }

}
```

Our resource is located at the root path of an application (1). In the first version, we have implemented the catalog as a `HashMap` and populated it with the first pet—`turtle` (2). The `searchById` method will be invoked when the `GET` method is invoked with the `"item"` address and the `itemId` parameter (3).

We can build and deploy the application as in the first chapter:

```
mvn wildfly-swarm:run
```

If we enter the address of the **catalog-service** in the web browser, we will be able to find our first pet in the catalog:

Fractions

In the preceding example, we did the following: we annotated our classes with JAX-RS annotations, built the code using Swarm Maven plugin, and obtained a runnable Swarm-based JAR. The resulting JAR is much smaller than a full application server. The reason for that is that Swarm has wrapped our code in only those parts of WildFly that it needs to work. Now, we will look in greater detail at this statement.

Let's run the application created in the preceding chapter again:

```
mvn wildfly-swarm:run
```

Let's look at the beginning of the console output:

```
INFO  [org.wildfly.extension.undertow] (ServerService Thread Pool -- 3) WFLYUT0022: Unregistered web context: '/' from server 'default-server'
INFO  [org.wildfly.extension.undertow] (MSC service thread 1-2) WFLYUT0008: Undertow HTTP listener default suspending
INFO  [org.wildfly.extension.undertow] (MSC service thread 1-2) WFLYUT0007: Undertow HTTP listener default stopped, was bound to [0:0:0:0:0:0:0:0]
INFO  [org.wildfly.extension.undertow] (MSC service thread 1-4) WFLYUT0019: Host default-host stopping
INFO  [org.wildfly.extension.undertow] (MSC service thread 1-4) WFLYUT0004: Undertow 1.4.18.Final stopping
INFO  [org.jboss.as.server.deployment] (MSC service thread 1-3) WFLYSRV0028: Stopped deployment example-catalog-service-1.0.war (runtime-name: exa
INFO  [org.jboss.as] (MSC service thread 1-5) WFLYSRV0050: WildFly Swarm 2018.3.0 (WildFly Core 3.0.8.Final) stopped in 24ms
-catalog-service]$ java -jar target/example-catalog-service-1.0-swarm.jar
INFO  [org.wildfly.swarm] (main) WFSWARM0013: Installed fraction:               Logging - STABLE         org.wildfly.swarm:logging:2018.3.0
INFO  [org.wildfly.swarm] (main) WFSWARM0013: Installed fraction:               Elytron - STABLE         org.wildfly.swarm:elytron:2018.3.0
INFO  [org.wildfly.swarm] (main) WFSWARM0013: Installed fraction:              Undertow - STABLE         org.wildfly.swarm:undertow:2018.3.0
INFO  [org.wildfly.swarm] (main) WFSWARM0013: Installed fraction:                JAX-RS - STABLE         org.wildfly.swarm:jaxrs:2018.3.0
INFO  [org.jboss.msc] (main) JBoss MSC version 1.2.7.SP1
INFO  [org.jboss.as] (MSC service thread 1-7) WFLYSRV0049: WildFly Swarm 2018.3.0 (WildFly Core 3.0.8.Final) starting
INFO  [org.wildfly.swarm] (MSC service thread 1-7) WFSWARM0015: Install MSC service for command line args: []
INFO  [org.wildfly.security] (ServerService Thread Pool -- 7) ELY00001: WildFly Elytron version 1.1.6.Final
INFO  [org.jboss.as.naming] (ServerService Thread Pool -- 12) WFLYNAM0001: Activating Naming Subsystem
INFO  [org.jboss.as.jaxrs] (ServerService Thread Pool -- 14) WFLYRS0016: RESTEasy version 3.0.24.Final
```

Take a look at the lines of the log in the red rectangle. Swarm is informing us that it has installed four fractions: JAX-RS, Undertow, Elytron, and Logging. However, what does it mean by that and what actually is a fraction?

The fraction is a part of the functionality needed by an application. To be more precise, fraction gathers the code and the configuration necessary for some part of the enterprise functionality to work.

As we have used JAX-RS in our service, we have added the JAX-RS fraction as a Maven dependency. To recall, this was the following dependency in the `pom.xml`:

```
(...)
        <dependency>
            <groupId>org.wildfly.swarm</groupId>
            <artifactId>jaxrs</artifactId>
            <version>${version.wildfly.swarm}</version>
        </dependency>

(...)
```

As a result, Swarm has built a service that contains this fraction. However, by looking again at the preceding screenshot, we can see that JAX-RS is not the only fraction installed as there are also Undertow, Elytron, and Logging fractions present.

The reason for the Logging fraction presence is that there are some fractions that are necessary for all configurations—logging is one among them. What about Undertow fraction? Fractions can depend on other fractions. As you probably know, JAX-RS needs to use a web server to serve web pages that it generates, and as a result, the JAX-RS fraction requires the dependency on the Undertow plugin. Swarm has discovered that we are using JAX-RS, so it included it in the generated application, but it also had to analyze dependencies of that fraction. The result of this analysis showed that another fraction, namely Undertow, has to be included. Similarly, both JAX-RS and Undertow depend on the Elytron fraction, which is responsible for implementing the security. As a result, it too was added to the created service.

Now, let's take a look at what happens if we decide to refactor our catalog service and use CDI.

 Examples reference: `chapter3/catalog-service-jaxrs-cdi/`.

Let's move the search functionality from the JAX-RS resource to the CDI service:

```
package org.packt.swarm.petstore.catalog;

import org.packt.swarm.petstore.catalog.model.Item;

import javax.enterprise.context.ApplicationScoped;
import java.util.HashMap;
import java.util.Map;

//1
@ApplicationScoped
public class CatalogService {

    private Map<String, Item> catalog = new HashMap<>();

    public CatalogService(){
        Item turtle = new Item();
        turtle.setItemId("turtle");
        turtle.setName("turtle");
        turtle.setQuantity(5);
        turtle.setDescription("Slow, friendly reptile. Let your busy self
```

```
    see how it spends 100 years of his life laying on sand and swimming.");
        catalog.put("turtle", turtle);
    }

    //2
    public Item searchById(String itemId){
        return catalog.get(itemId);
    }

}
```

We created an application-scoped bean (1) and provided the Search method as the part of its API (2). Also, we have to modify the CatalogResource:

```
package org.packt.swarm.petstore.catalog;

import org.packt.swarm.petstore.catalog.model.Item;

import javax.inject.Inject;
import javax.ws.rs.GET;
import javax.ws.rs.Path;
import javax.ws.rs.PathParam;
import javax.ws.rs.Produces;
import javax.ws.rs.core.MediaType;
import javax.ws.rs.core.Response;

@Path("/")
public class CatalogResource {

    //1
    @Inject
    private CatalogService catalogService;

    @GET
    @Path("item/{itemId}")
    @Produces(MediaType.APPLICATION_JSON)
    public Response searchByName(@PathParam("itemId") String itemId) {
        try {
            //2
            Item item = catalogService.searchById(itemId);
            return Response.ok(item).build();
        } catch (Exception e) {
            return
```

```
Response.status(Response.Status.BAD_REQUEST).entity(e.getMessage()).build()
;
        }
    }

}
```

We injected the `CatalogService` that we have just created to it (1) and used it to look for the pet (2). Finally, we have to modify the `pom.xml`:

```
(...)

    <dependencies>
        <dependency>
            <groupId>org.wildfly.swarm</groupId>
            <artifactId>jaxrs</artifactId>
            <version>${version.wildfly.swarm}</version>
        </dependency>
        <!-- 1 -->
        <dependency>
            <groupId>org.wildfly.swarm</groupId>
            <artifactId>cdi</artifactId>
            <version>${version.wildfly.swarm}</version>
        </dependency>

    </dependencies>

(...)
```

We have to add Swarm's CDI fraction (2).

After doing all of the things mentioned previously in this chapter, we can build our application and see a result that is similar to the one in the preceding example.

Let's look at the WildFly-Swarm plugin's log again:

```
UT0019: Host default-host stopping
UT0004: Undertow 1.4.18.Final stopping
SRV0028: Stopped deployment catalog-service-1.0.war (runtime-name: catalog-service-1.0.war)
warm 2018.3.0 (WildFly Core 3.0.8.Final) stopped in 38ms
atalog-service-1.0-swarm.jar
          Logging - STABLE          org.wildfly.swarm:logging:2018.3.0
  Bean Validation - STABLE          org.wildfly.swarm:bean-validation:2018.3.0
CDI Configuration - STABLE          org.wildfly.swarm:cdi-config:2018.3.0
          Elytron - STABLE          org.wildfly.swarm:elytron:2018.3.0
              CDI - STABLE          org.wildfly.swarm:cdi:2018.3.0
     Transactions - STABLE          org.wildfly.swarm:transactions:2018.3.0
         Undertow - STABLE          org.wildfly.swarm:undertow:2018.3.0
           JAX-RS - STABLE          org.wildfly.swarm:jaxrs:2018.3.0

warm 2018.3.0 (WildFly Core 3.0.8.Final) starting
all MSC service for command line args: []
001. WildFly Elytron version 1.1.6.Final
```

We now have eight fractions present. Apart from the ones that were introduced in the preceding application, CDI, CDI-config, `Bean Validation`, and `Transactions` have been added. Again, Swarm has scanned the application and found out that it relies on JAX-RS and CDI; it has added those fractions and all their dependencies.

As you probably noted, the fractions that we see now are tightly related to Java EE specification. Can we then think of them as particular Java EE specification implementations added to the server core on demand? No. As we already know, Swarm is based on the Java EE server and part of its use case is to enable the transition from the monolith applications to microservices, there is a large group of fractions that map to the implementation of some Java EE functionalities. They are not limited to that, though. There is another group of fractions that provide functionality outside the Java EE. What is more, you are also able to implement your own fraction if you need it in your use case.

Look under WildFly's hood to understand how WildFly plugin works internally to create your lean Swarm application. Let's start by explaining how fraction detection works and how you can change its behavior by modifying Swarm's configuration parameters.

Fraction detection

Let's return to our latest `CatalogService`. As you recall, it uses JAX-RS and CDI. We have provided the dependencies manually by editing the `pom.xml` file:

```
(...)

    <dependencies>
        <!-- 1 -->
        <dependency>
            <groupId>org.wildfly.swarm</groupId>
            <artifactId>jaxrs</artifactId>
            <version>${version.wildfly.swarm}</version>
        </dependency>

        <!-- 2 -->
        <dependency>
            <groupId>org.wildfly.swarm</groupId>
            <artifactId>cdi</artifactId>
            <version>${version.wildfly.swarm}</version>
        </dependency>
    </dependencies>

(...)
```

We have provided dependencies for two fractions: JAX-RS (1) and CDI (2). We can run the application and note that it is indeed working.

Let's continue our experiment now. What happens if we configure only one fraction?

```
(...)
<dependencyManagement>
    <dependencies>
        <!-- 2 -->
        <dependency>
            <groupId>org.jboss.spec</groupId>
            <artifactId>jboss-javaee-7.0</artifactId>
            <version>${version.jboss.spec.javaee.7.0}</version>
            <type>pom</type>
            <scope>import</scope>
        </dependency>
    </dependencies>
</dependencyManagement>

<dependencies>
    <!-- 1 -->
    <dependency>
```

```xml
                <groupId>org.wildfly.swarm</groupId>
                <artifactId>jaxrs</artifactId>
                <version>${version.wildfly.swarm}</version>
            </dependency>

            <!-- 2 -->
            <dependency>
                <groupId>javax.enterprise</groupId>
                <artifactId>cdi-api</artifactId>
                <scope>provided</scope>
            </dependency>
        </dependencies>
```
```
    </dependencies>
```

```
(...)
```

In the preceding code, only the JAX-RS dependency is configured (1). Note that in such a case we have to explicitly define a dependency on CDI-API (2). When we run the application, we see the following log:

```
: Installed fraction:                       Logging - STABLE        org.wildfly.swarm:logging:2018.3.0
: Installed fraction:                       Elytron - STABLE        org.wildfly.swarm:elytron:2018.3.0
: Installed fraction:                      Undertow - STABLE        org.wildfly.swarm:undertow:2018.3.0
: Installed fraction:                        JAX-RS - STABLE        org.wildfly.swarm:jaxrs:2018.3.0
on 1.2.7.SP1
) WFLYSRV0049: WildFly Swarm 2018.3.0 (WildFly Core 3.0.8.Final) starting
1 1-7) WFSWARM0019: Install MSC service for command line args: []
Thread Pool -- 3) ELY00001: WildFly Elytron version 1.1.6.Final
ead Pool -- 14) WFLYRS0016: RESTEasy version 3.0.24.Final
Thread Pool -- 16) WFLYSEC0002: Activating Security Subsystem
```

You will see no errors yet, but the first few lines of your log already foretell that problems will occur. Although CDI is used, its fractions (and its dependents) have not been added. If we get into a browser and enter the address of our service, we will see a bad request error. Add a temporary log to service class:

```java
package org.packt.swarm.petstore.catalog;

import org.jboss.logging.Logger;
import org.packt.swarm.petstore.catalog.model.Item;

import javax.inject.Inject;
import javax.ws.rs.GET;
import javax.ws.rs.Path;
import javax.ws.rs.PathParam;
import javax.ws.rs.Produces;
import javax.ws.rs.core.MediaType;
import javax.ws.rs.core.Response;

@Path("/")
```

```
public class CatalogResource {

    private final Logger log = Logger.getLogger(getClass());

    @Inject
    private CatalogService catalogService;

    @GET
    @Path("item/{itemId}")
    @Produces(MediaType.APPLICATION_JSON)
    public Response searchByName(@PathParam("itemId") String itemId) {
        try {
            Item item = catalogService.searchById(itemId);
            return Response.ok(item).build();
        } catch (Exception e) {
            log.error("BAD REQUEST", e);
            return
Response.status(Response.Status.BAD_REQUEST).entity(e.getMessage()).build()
;
        }
    }

}
```

We will be able to note the cause of our problem:

```
ERROR [org.packt.swarm.petstore.catalog.CatalogResource] (default task-1)
Bad request: java.lang.NullPointerException
        at
org.packt.swarm.petstore.catalog.CatalogResource.searchByName(CatalogResour
ce.java:27)
        at sun.reflect.NativeMethodAccessorImpl.invoke0(Native Method)
        at
sun.reflect.NativeMethodAccessorImpl.invoke(NativeMethodAccessorImpl.java:6
2)
        at
sun.reflect.DelegatingMethodAccessorImpl.invoke(DelegatingMethodAccessorImp
l.java:43)
        at java.lang.reflect.Method.invoke(Method.java:498)
        at
org.jboss.resteasy.core.MethodInjectorImpl.invoke(MethodInjectorImpl.java:1
40)
        at
org.jboss.resteasy.core.ResourceMethodInvoker.invokeOnTarget(ResourceMethod
Invoker.java:295)
        at
org.jboss.resteasy.core.ResourceMethodInvoker.invoke(ResourceMethodInvoker.
java:249)
```

```
        at
org.jboss.resteasy.core.ResourceMethodInvoker.invoke(ResourceMethodInvoker.
java:236)
        at
org.jboss.resteasy.core.SynchronousDispatcher.invoke(SynchronousDispatcher.
java:406)
        at
org.jboss.resteasy.core.SynchronousDispatcher.invoke(SynchronousDispatcher.
java:213)
        at
org.jboss.resteasy.plugins.server.servlet.ServletContainerDispatcher.servic
e(ServletContainerDispatcher.java:228)
        at
org.jboss.resteasy.plugins.server.servlet.HttpServletDispatcher.service(Htt
pServletDispatcher.java:56)
        at
org.jboss.resteasy.plugins.server.servlet.HttpServletDispatcher.service(Htt
pServletDispatcher.java:51)
        at javax.servlet.http.HttpServlet.service(HttpServlet.java:790)
```

Owing to missing CDI fraction, bean resolution and injection were not performed. As a result, the service object was not injected into the `CatalogResource` resource, resulting in `NullPointerException`.

Let's get one step further and remove all the fractions:

```
<dependencies>
    <!-- 2 -->
    <dependency>
        <groupId>org.jboss.spec.javax.ws.rs</groupId>
        <artifactId>jboss-jaxrs-api_2.0_spec</artifactId>
        <scope>provided</scope>
    </dependency>
    <dependency>
        <groupId>javax.enterprise</groupId>
        <artifactId>cdi-api</artifactId>
        <scope>provided</scope>
    </dependency>
    <!-- 1 -->
    <!-- no fractions here ... -->
</dependencies>

(...)
```

We have removed all the fractions (1). Please note that in such a case we have to provide all of the Java EE APIs manually (2).

 Example reference: `chapter3/catalog-service-auto-detect/`.

When we build the project configured this way, we will see something interesting in the log:

```
[INFO] Processing war project
[INFO] Webapp assembled in [14 msecs]
[INFO] Building war: /home/tomek/książka/swarm-examples/example-catalog-service/target/catalog-servi
ce-1.0.war
[INFO]
[INFO] --- wildfly-swarm-plugin:2018.3.0:package (default) @ catalog-service ---
[INFO] Scanning for needed WildFly Swarm fractions with mode: when missing
[INFO] Detected fractions: cdi:2018.3.0, jaxrs:2018.3.0
[INFO] Adding fractions: bean-validation:2018.3.0, cdi-config:2018.3.0, cdi:2018.3.0, container:2018
3.0, ee:2018.3.0, jaxrs-cdi:2018.3.0, jaxrs:2018.3.0, logging:2018.3.0, security:2018.3.0, transact
ions:2018.3.0, undertow:2018.3.0
Resolving 59 out of 273 artifacts
[INFO] Repackaging .war: /home/tomek/książka/swarm-examples/example-catalog-service/target/catalog-s
ervice-1.0.war
[INFO] Repackaged .war: /home/tomek/książka/swarm-examples/example-catalog-service/target/catalog-se
rvice-1.0.war
[INFO]
[INFO] --- maven-install-plugin:2.4:install (default-install) @ catalog-service ---
```

In the preceding example, Swarm has performed automatic fraction detection. How does it work?

Swarm found out that `org.packt.swarm.petstore.catalog.CatalogResource` is using the classes from the `javax.ws.rs` package, which resulted in the inclusion of JAX-RS. Similarly, usage of the `javax.inject` package led to the inclusion of the CDI fraction. Later, as in manual examples, Swarm has a build service that contains the detected fractions, their dependencies, and fractions that are always needed. If you run the service now, you will note that it is indeed working correctly.

In order to understand why Swarm behaved in the described way in the recent examples, we must learn about fraction detection mode. Let's do it now.

Fraction detection mode

Swarm Maven plugin can work in different fraction detection modes. If you do not provide fraction dependencies manually, it runs in the when-missing mode. We have already seen the behavior of this mode in our previous examples: when no direct fraction dependency is provided, the plugin performs auto-detection. On the other hand, if we provide at least one fraction dependency manually, the auto-detection mode is turned off. This is the reason why our last example wasn't built with the CDI fraction included: adding the JAX-RS fraction manually turned auto-detection off.

Is there something we can do about it? Yup, we can use a different detection mode: `force`. This mode makes auto-detection work every time. After detecting the fractions that are used, it merges the detection result with fractions configured by the user.

 Example reference: `chapter3/catalog-service-force-detect`.

Let's reconfigure our example to make it work:

```
(...)

<dependencies>
    <dependency>
        <groupId>javax.enterprise</groupId>
        <artifactId>cdi-api</artifactId>
        <scope>provided</scope>
    </dependency>
    <!-- 1 -->
    <dependency>
        <groupId>org.wildfly.swarm</groupId>
        <artifactId>jaxrs</artifactId>
        <version>${version.wildfly.swarm}</version>
    </dependency>
</dependencies>

<build>
    <plugins>
        <plugin>
            <artifactId>maven-war-plugin</artifactId>
            <version>${version.war.plugin}</version>
            <configuration>
                <failOnMissingWebXml>false</failOnMissingWebXml>
            </configuration>
```

```
            </plugin>
            <plugin>
                <groupId>org.wildfly.swarm</groupId>
                <artifactId>wildfly-swarm-plugin</artifactId>
                <version>${version.wildfly.swarm}</version>
                <!-- 2 -->
                <configuration>
                    <fractionDetectMode>force</fractionDetectMode>
                </configuration>
                <executions>
                    <execution>
                        <goals>
                            <goal>package</goal>
                        </goals>
                    </execution>
                </executions>
            </plugin>
        </plugins>
    </build>

</project>
```

Again, only the JAX-RS fraction is configured (1); however, because we have configured the Maven plugin with the `force` detection mode (2), Swarm will also detect the previously missing CDI fraction. If we run our application again, we will see that all necessary fractions were detected and the application works correctly.

We have seen two fraction detection modes: when-missing and `force`. Is there another? Yes, there is one more: *never*. In this mode, as its name implies, the fractions are never detected, and you always have to provide all of them manually.

Thin and hollow JARs

As we said before, during the standard Maven plugin operation, the resulting application contains both the Swarm server and the application that is deployed on it. We can change that behavior. Let's suppose that we deploy our application in the cloud and later push new changes to its code. Since it is the application code that changes in most cases, we would like to create the container with the server in the cloud and later push only code to it. How are we able to do it? By using hollow JARs.

Using hollow JARs

You are able to configure the Maven plugin to build hollow JARs, which contain the swarm server without the actual application deployed on it. Let's return to the JAX-RS + CDI example again to show how it works.

 Example reference: `chapter3/catalog-service-hollow-jar`.

The first thing that we will need to do is configure the Maven plugin:

```
( ... )

    <build>
        <plugins>
            <plugin>
                <artifactId>maven-war-plugin</artifactId>
                <version>${version.war.plugin}</version>
                <configuration>
                    <failOnMissingWebXml>false</failOnMissingWebXml>
                </configuration>
            </plugin>
            <plugin>
                <groupId>org.wildfly.swarm</groupId>
                <artifactId>wildfly-swarm-plugin</artifactId>
                <version>${version.wildfly.swarm}</version>
                <!-- 1 -->
                <configuration>
                    <hollow>true</hollow>
                </configuration>
                <executions>
                    <execution>
                        <goals>
                            <goal>package</goal>
                        </goals>
                    </execution>
                </executions>
            </plugin>
        </plugins>
    </build>
( ... )
```

The only thing that we have to do is to enable the hollow configuration parameter (1). When we build the application and navigate to our target directory, we will see the following output:

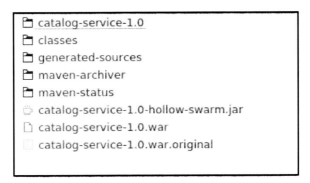

As you can see in the preceding screenshot, one directory ends with the -hollow-swarm suffix. This is our hollow jar without the deployed application. When running it, we must provide the name of the application that we will deploy on the created server. We will be able to do it in the following way:

```
java jar catalog-1.0-hollow-swarm.jar catalog-1.0.war
```

This will start the container and run our application. As a result, it will behave in the same way as the original example.

Using thin JARs

You will be able to create a thin JAR. A thin JAR does not contain its Maven dependencies and loads them during application startup from a local or remote Maven repository.

Example reference: chapter3/catalog-service-thin-jar.

Let's take a look at an example:

```
(...)

    <build>
        <plugins>
            <plugin>
                <artifactId>maven-war-plugin</artifactId>
                <version>${version.war.plugin}</version>
                <configuration>
                    <failOnMissingWebXml>false</failOnMissingWebXml>
                </configuration>
            </plugin>
            <plugin>
                <groupId>org.wildfly.swarm</groupId>
                <artifactId>wildfly-swarm-plugin</artifactId>
                <version>${version.wildfly.swarm}</version>
                <!-- 1 -->
                <configuration>
                    <bundleDependencies>false</bundleDependencies>
                </configuration>
                <executions>
                    <execution>
                        <goals>
                            <goal>package</goal>
                        </goals>
                    </execution>
                </executions>
            </plugin>
        </plugins>
    </build>

(...)
```

When we build the application and look at the target directory, we get the following result:

```
14M       catalog-service-1.0
744K      catalog-service-1.0-swarm.jar
8,0K      catalog-service-1.0.war
12M       catalog-service-1.0.war.original
44K       classes
8,0K      generated-sources
8,0K      maven-archiver
24K       maven-status
```

Note that in the preceding scenario, all the JARs are very small with the runnable JAR of `744` KB.

You also have the possibility to mix thin JARs with hollow JARs. The runnable JAR does not contain the application that has to be deployed on it, so it has to be run in the same way as in the preceding example:

```
java jar catalog-1.0-hollow-swarm.jar catalog-1.0.war
```

Both the server and the deployment do not contain bundled dependencies, so they have to be loaded from the Maven repository using the application deployment.

Summary

In this chapter, you learned how Swarm creates runnable, right-sized services. You learned what a fraction is, how the fraction detection process looks, and how you can modify it. Finally, you learned how to create hollow and thin JARs.

In the next chapter, we will show you how to configure your microservices.

4
Tuning the Configuration of Your Services

In this chapter, you will learn how to configure your Swarm services. We will show you practical examples of different configuration tools that are available and how you can use them to steer the behavior of your applications.

Modifying Swarm configuration

The fractions available in Swarm come with reasonable defaults. In the examples that we have seen so far, we didn't touch any configuration and yet we were able to see the applications working. Now, we will show you how you can tune the configuration of Swarm-created services.

Swarm provides a set of tools that allows you to modify the configuration of your applications. In the following section, we will introduce them one by one and show their usage in different scenarios. Let's start with the simplest one: system properties.

System properties

You are able to modify the configuration by specifying system properties. Let's return to our **catalog-service**. As you saw in the **catalog-service** examples from the last chapter, the JAX-RS application was listening for HTTP requests on port 8080, which is the default configuration. Let's suppose that we want to change that port.

What we have to do is specify the `swarm.http.port` property during the application execution, as follows:

```
mvn clean wildfly-swarm:run -Dswarm.http.port=12345
```

When running the web browser, we can see that, indeed, the port on which the application runs has been changed:

What has just happened here then? The undertow fraction has discovered that there is a configuration property that overrides the standard HTTP port, and it modifies the socket's configuration accordingly. As a result, the running application is using the specified port.

Each fraction contains a group of properties that can be used to configure it. You will be able to find them in Swarm documentation.

The method of editing the properties is very simple and can be sufficient in many cases, but the entry point to the more complex programmatic configurations may be more feasible let's learn how to do it.

Implementing your own main class

Each Swarm service contains the `main` class which is responsible for creating and configuring a runtime for the service and running service code on it. Swarm creates the default implementation of the `main` class (in fact, the default class was used in all the examples till now), but you are able to provide your own implementation of the `Main` class if you want to modify the default behavior. An example of such modification may be providing an additional configuration.

Let's return to the **catalog-service**. Let's recall its current operation: we created a `jaxrs` resource and injected the service providing the invitation message using CDI. Now, let's modify this example to provide our own `main` class.

Examples reference: `chapter4/catalog-service-first-main`

In order to do it, we have to modify the `pom.xml` of the **catalog-service** in the following way:

```
(...)

    <dependencies>
        <!-- 2 -->
        <dependency>
            <groupId>org.wildfly.swarm</groupId>
            <artifactId>jaxrs</artifactId>
            <version>${version.wildfly.swarm}</version>
        </dependency>
        <dependency>
            <groupId>org.wildfly.swarm</groupId>
            <artifactId>cdi</artifactId>
            <version>${version.wildfly.swarm}</version>
        </dependency>
    </dependencies>

    <build>
        <plugins>
            <plugin>
                <artifactId>maven-war-plugin</artifactId>
                <version>${version.war.plugin}</version>
                <configuration>
                    <failOnMissingWebXml>false</failOnMissingWebXml>
                </configuration>
            </plugin>
            <plugin>
                <groupId>org.wildfly.swarm</groupId>
                <artifactId>wildfly-swarm-plugin</artifactId>
                <version>${version.wildfly.swarm}</version>
                <!-- 1 -->
                <configuration>
                    <mainClass>org.packt.swarm.petstore.catalog.Main</mainClass>
                </configuration>
                <executions>
                    <execution>
                        <phase>package</phase>
                        <goals>
                            <goal>package</goal>
                        </goals>
```

```
                    </execution>
                </executions>
            </plugin>
        </plugins>
    </build>

</project>
```

We have to modify the Swarm plugin so that its configuration contains the class with our `main` method (1). When using your own `main` method, you have to specify manually on which fractions your service depends (2).

Now, let's take a look at the `org.packt.swarm.petstore.Main` class, which implements the `main` method:

```
package org.packt.swarm.petstore.catalog;

import org.jboss.logging.Logger;
import org.wildfly.swarm.Swarm;

public class Main {

    public static void main(String[] args) throws Exception {
        //1
        new Swarm().start().deploy();
        //2
        Logger.getLogger(Main.class).info("I'M HERE!");
    }

}
```

We created the instance of the `org.wildfly.swarm.Swarm` class (1). The `start` method has created the container, and the `deploy` method has deployed the created archive on it. We have also created (2) the log output to prove that the class is indeed working. We will look at the `Swarm` class in greater detail in just a moment, but before that here is the mentioned proof:

```
INFO  [org.jboss.weld.deployer] (MSC service thread 1-4) WFLYWELD0003: Processing weld deployment catalog-service-1.0.war
INFO  [org.hibernate.validator.internal.util.Version] (MSC service thread 1-4) HV000001: Hibernate Validator 5.3.5.Final
INFO  [org.jboss.weld.Version] (MSC service thread 1-8) WELD-000900: 2.4.3 (Final)
INFO  [org.wildfly.extension.undertow] (MSC service thread 1-7) WFLYUT0018: Host default-host starting
INFO  [org.jboss.resteasy.resteasy_jaxrs.i18n] (ServerService Thread Pool -- 7) RESTEASY002225: Deploying javax.ws.rs.core.Application
INFO  [org.wildfly.extension.undertow] (ServerService Thread Pool -- 7) WFLYUT0021: Registered web context: '/' for server 'default-se
INFO  [org.jboss.as.server] (main) WFLYSRV0010: Deployed "catalog-service-1.0.war" (runtime-name : "catalog-service-1.0.war")
INFO  [org.packt.swarm.petstore.catalog.Main] (main) I'M HERE!
INFO  [org.wildfly.swarm] (main) WFSWARM99999: WildFly Swarm is Ready
```

The message is there, and the method has been executed.

The Swarm class

As we have seen in the preceding section, if you are implementing your own `main` method, you will interact with the `org.wildfly.swarm.Swarm` class. This class is responsible for instantiating the container based on the provided configuration and creating and deploying the archive with your application. Both of those steps can be modified by operations on the `Swarm` class. Let's learn more about them.

Providing the configuration

The `Swarm` class provides a group of methods that allow you to modify the configuration using the Java API, such as `fraction`, `socketBinding`, and `outboundSocketBinding`. The latter two methods, as their names imply, allow you to create your own socket binding and outbound socket binding groups. The method that is the most interesting to us is the `fraction` method. It takes one argument for the `org.wildfly.swarm.spi.api.Fraction` class implementations—the `fraction`. You will be able to modify and reconfigure all the fractions and provide them to Swarm. Let's get a first grasp of this functionality on our favorite example, that is, changing the HTTP port of the `CatalogService`.

 Examples reference: `chapter4/catalog-service-config-main`

Firstly, we have to add the `UndertowFraction` dependency to our `pom.xml`:

```
(...)

    <dependencies>
        <dependency>
            <groupId>org.jboss.spec.javax.ws.rs</groupId>
            <artifactId>jboss-jaxrs-api_2.0_spec</artifactId>
            <scope>provided</scope>
        </dependency>
        <dependency>
            <groupId>javax.enterprise</groupId>
            <artifactId>cdi-api</artifactId>
            <scope>provided</scope>
        </dependency>
        <dependency>
            <groupId>org.wildfly.swarm</groupId>
            <artifactId>jaxrs</artifactId>
```

```xml
            <version>${version.wildfly.swarm}</version>
        </dependency>
        <dependency>
            <groupId>org.wildfly.swarm</groupId>
            <artifactId>cdi</artifactId>
            <version>${version.wildfly.swarm}</version>
        </dependency>
        <!-- 1 -->
        <dependency>
            <groupId>org.wildfly.swarm</groupId>
            <artifactId>undertow</artifactId>
            <version>${version.wildfly.swarm}</version>
        </dependency>
        <dependency>
            <groupId>org.jboss.logging</groupId>
            <artifactId>jboss-logging</artifactId>
            <version>3.3.0.Final</version>
            <scope>provided</scope>
        </dependency>

    </dependencies>

(...)
```

Secondly, let's reimplement the main method:

```java
package org.packt.swarm.petstore.catalog;

import org.wildfly.swarm.Swarm;
import org.wildfly.swarm.undertow.UndertowFraction;

public class Main {

    public static void main(String[] args) throws Exception {
        //1
        UndertowFraction undertowFraction = new UndertowFraction();
        //2
        undertowFraction.applyDefaults();
        //3
        undertowFraction.httpPort(12345);
        //4
        Swarm swarm = new Swarm();
        //5
        swarm.fraction(undertowFraction);
        //6
        swarm.start().deploy();
    }
}
```

If you run the preceding code, you will indeed see the same result as in the property example: the application is running on the `12345` port. So, what has just happened?

At the beginning of the preceding code, we created the `UndertowFraction` (1) and run the `applyDefaults` method (2). If the `fraction` is automatically created by Swarm, the default configuration is applied to it. On the other hand, if you create the `fraction` manually, you are creating the empty `fraction` object with no configuration. That's what the `applyDefaults` method is for. It applies the default configuration to the `fraction` object. As a result, whenever you don't want to create the configuration from scratch and just modify it, you have to invoke the `applyDefaults` method first and apply your configuration changes after that. That's exactly the scenario in our simple example. We didn't want to create the full configuration manually. Instead, we only wanted to change the one configuration parameter—the listening port. As a result, we applied the default configuration to the `fraction` object, and after that, we only changed the HTTP port.

We created the `UndertowFraction` object that represents the configuration of the Undertow fraction. We have to provide this configuration to the container that will run the service. In order to do it, we used Swarm's `fraction` method (4). It is worth mentioning here that the application still consists of many `fractions` but we have provided only the `Undertowfraction` configuration. If we don't add a customized `fraction` configuration to the `Swarm` class, then the default configuration is used. Swarm is still going to bootstrap CDI and JAX-RS among others, but their configuration will be created automatically, just as it was in our first example. On the other hand, the `Undertowconfiguration` object is provided by us manually and Swarm will use it.

After the application is configured, we are ready to start and deploy (5) it, just as we did in the previous example. If we run our application, we will see the same result that we obtained in the example that used the system property—the application runs on port `12345`.

However, in the property example, we have to add only one configuration parameter, and, here, we have to do quite a lot of stuff. You may ask whether you can use the Java API to provide a more elaborate configuration but still resort to the properties in cases such as an HTTP port; that's a good question. Let's find out.

Using your own main along with properties

Let's modify the Main class to the simplest possible form:

```
package org.packt.swarm.petstore;

import org.jboss.logging.Logger;
import org.wildfly.swarm.Swarm;

public class Main {

    public static void main(String[] args) throws Exception {
        new Swarm().start().deploy();
    }
}
```

Then, run it with the HTTP port property:

```
mvn clean wildfly-swarm:run -Dswarm.http.port=12345
```

Also, we will check in in the browser:

Well, it didn't work. So, as it just turned out, you are not able to do it, sorry.

I am kidding, of course. You can do it, but as it turned out, we have, completely accidentally, made a small mistake in our code from the last listing. What is wrong with it? The system properties with which the main method was executed were not propagated to Swarm in any way. Consider that, on the other hand, we have written our code in the following way:

```
package org.packt.swarm.petstore;

import org.jboss.logging.Logger;
import org.wildfly.swarm.Swarm;

public class Main {

  public static void main(String[] args) throws Exception {
```

```
//1
new Swarm(args).start().deploy();
Logger.getLogger(Main.class).info("I'M HERE!");
    }
}
```

The application will use specified properties and present the application behavior we will be able to see that it is working correctly.

To sum up, you are now able to mix the Java API with a properties-based configuration, but you have to remember to create Swarm with `main` function arguments.

Java API

Let's return to the `Swarm` class. We have already seen that we are able to create the fraction class with our own configuration and hand it on to the `Swarm` class. In fact, we are able to steer the whole Swarm configuration programmatically. To create a more elaborate example, let's extend our `CatalogService` so that it stores its data in a database.

 Examples reference: `chapter4/catalog-service-database`.

Let's start with editing the `pom.xml`:

```
(...)

    <properties>
        (...)
        <version.hibernate.api>1.0.0.Final</version.hibernate.api>
        <version.h2>1.4.187</version.h2>
    </properties>

    (...)

    <dependencies>
        (...)
        <dependency>
            <groupId>org.wildfly.swarm</groupId>
            <artifactId>cdi</artifactId>
            <version>${version.wildfly.swarm}</version>
        </dependency>
        //1
```

```
            <dependency>
                <groupId>org.wildfly.swarm</groupId>
                <artifactId>datasources</artifactId>
                <version>${version.wildfly.swarm}</version>
            </dependency>
            //2
            <dependency>
                <groupId>org.wildfly.swarm</groupId>
                <artifactId>jpa</artifactId>
                <version>${version.wildfly.swarm}</version>
            </dependency>
            //3
            <dependency>
                <groupId>org.hibernate.javax.persistence</groupId>
                <artifactId>hibernate-jpa-2.1-api</artifactId>
                <version>${version.hibernate.api}</version>
            </dependency>
            //4
            <dependency>
                <groupId>com.h2database</groupId>
                <artifactId>h2</artifactId>
                <version>${version.h2}</version>
            </dependency>

    </dependencies>

    (...)

</project>
```

We have added four new Maven dependencies. In order to configure our own `datasource`, we have to add the `datasources` fraction (1). As we will use the Java Persistence API, we will need both the `jpa` fraction and the JPA API (2). We will also use `h2` in-memory database, and we need its `dependency` too (3). Finally, we provide the `dependency` to `h2` database (4).

As we are going to persist the data about pets available in the store, we have to modify the `Item` class so that it is an entity, a JPA object representing a state that will be persisted in the relational database:

```
package org.packt.swarm.petstore.catalog.model;

import com.fasterxml.jackson.annotation.JsonIgnore;

import javax.persistence.Column;
import javax.persistence.Entity;
```

```
import javax.persistence.Id;
import javax.persistence.NamedQueries;
import javax.persistence.NamedQuery;
import javax.persistence.Table;

//1
@Entity
//2
@Table(name = "item")
//3
@NamedQueries({
        @NamedQuery(name="Item.findById",
                query="SELECT i FROM Item i WHERE i.itemId = :itemId"),
})
public class Item {

    //4
    @Id
    @JsonIgnore
    private int id;

    //5
    @Column(length = 30)
    private String itemId;

    //6
    @Column(length = 30)
    private String name;
    @Column
    private int quantity;

    @Column
    private String description;

    public String getItemId() {
        return itemId;
    }

    public void setItemId(String itemId) {
        this.itemId = itemId;
    }

    public String getName() {
        return name;
    }

    public void setName(String name) {
        this.name = name;
```

```
    }

    public int getQuantity() {
        return quantity;
    }

    public void setQuantity(int quantity) {
        this.quantity = quantity;
    }

    public String getDescription() {
        return description;
    }

    public void setDescription(String description) {
        this.description = description;
    }
}
```

This is a simple jpa entity (1) with the corresponding table named "ITEM" (2). We have created the NamedQuery (3) to find pets by name. We have added the database ID field (4). Furthermore, we have added the @Column annotations so that name and quantity fields are persisted to the database (5).

We would also need to modify our CatalogService class so that it can load pet data from the database:

```
package org.packt.swarm.petstore.catalog;

import org.packt.swarm.petstore.catalog.model.Item;

import javax.enterprise.context.ApplicationScoped;
import javax.persistence.EntityManager;
import javax.persistence.PersistenceContext;


@ApplicationScoped
public class CatalogService {

    //1
    @PersistenceContext(unitName = "CatalogPU")
    private EntityManager em;

    //2
```

```
        public Item searchById(String itemId) {
            return em.createNamedQuery("Item.findById",
    Item.class).setParameter("itemId", itemId).getSingleResult();
    >       }


    }
```

We referenced the `CatalogPU` persistence context (we will configure it in a moment) and used a named query defined in an `Item` class to find pets by `id` (2).

OK, let's move to the interesting part. We will create and use in-memory `h2 datasource`; The following is the code to do so:

```
package org.packt.swarm.petstore.catalog;

import org.wildfly.swarm.Swarm;
import org.wildfly.swarm.datasources.DatasourcesFraction;

public class Main {

    public static void main(String[] args) throws Exception {
        DatasourcesFraction datasourcesFraction = new DatasourcesFraction()
                //1
                .jdbcDriver("h2", (d) -> {
                    d.driverClassName("org.h2.Driver");
                    d.xaDatasourceClass("org.h2.jdbcx.JdbcDataSource");
                    d.driverModuleName("com.h2database.h2");
                })
                //2
                .dataSource("CatalogDS", (ds) -> {
                    ds.driverName("h2");
ds.connectionUrl("jdbc:h2:mem:test;DB_CLOSE_DELAY=-1;DB_CLOSE_ON_EXIT=FALSE
");
                    ds.userName("sa");
                    ds.password("sa");
                });

        Swarm swarm = new Swarm();
        swarm.fraction(datasourcesFraction);
        swarm.start().deploy();
    }
}
```

The configuration of the `datasourcesFraction` is a bit more complex than the simple port change—let's look at it in greater detail. In (1), we defined the **Java Database Connectivity (JDBC)** driver named `"h2"` and provided lambda expression implementing the `org.wildfly.swarm.config.JDBCDriverConsumer` class—this is basically the acceptor that allows you to apply the additional configuration to the created JDBC driver. The analogous situation happens in (2). Here, we created the `CatalogDS` datasource and applied an additional configuration using the `org.wildfly.swarm.config.DatasourcesConsumer` class.

As you can see in the preceding code, this configuration is not as trivial as the `Undertowport` change, but don't worry. Swarm comes with the current Java API library with each release, and as all the configuration options are described there, you don't have to rely on guesswork while configuring your application using this method [1].

We still have to do more things to make our example work, such as provide `persistence.xml` and fill our database with a group of messages on startup.

Let's start with the first thing. The following is our `persistence.xml` file:

```xml
<?xml version="1.0" encoding="UTF-8"?>
<persistence
        xmlns:xsi="http://www.w3.org/2001/XMLSchema-instance"
        version="2.1"
        xmlns="http://xmlns.jcp.org/xml/ns/persistence"
        xsi:schemaLocation="http://xmlns.jcp.org/xml/ns/persistence
http://xmlns.jcp.org/xml/ns/persistence/persistence_2_1.xsd">
    <!-- 1 -->
    <persistence-unit name="CatalogPU" transaction-type="JTA">
        <!-- 2 -->
        <jta-data-source>java:jboss/datasources/CatalogDS</jta-data-source>
        <properties>
            <!-- 3 -->
            <property name="javax.persistence.schema-
generation.database.action" value="drop-and-create"/>
            <property name="javax.persistence.schema-generation.create-
source" value="metadata"/>
            <property name="javax.persistence.schema-generation.drop-
source" value="metadata"/>
            <!-- 4 -->
            <property name="javax.persistence.sql-load-script-source"
value="META-INF/load.sql"/>
        </properties>
    </persistence-unit>
</persistence>
```

In the preceding configuration, we created the persistent-unit named `CatalogPU`, which uses `JTA` transactions (1), made the persistent-unit use the `CatalogDS` datasource created earlier (2), provided a configuration that will make the database create the new database on the deployment and delete it on undeployment using entity classes metadata (3), and, finally, provided the load script (4).

The problem is that we don't have it yet; let's add it then:

```
INSERT INTO ITEM(id, itemId, name, description, quantity) VALUES (1,
'turtle', 'turtle',  'Slow friendly reptile. Let your busy self see how it
spends a hundred years of his life laying on sand and swimming.', 5);
INSERT INTO ITEM(id, itemId, name, description, quantity) VALUES (2,
'hamster', 'hamster', 'Energetic rodent - great as a first pet. Will be
your only inmate that takes his fitness training seriously.', 10);
INSERT INTO ITEM(id, itemId, name, description, quantity) VALUES (3,
'goldfish', 'goldfish', 'With its beauty it will be the decoration of you
aquarium. Likes gourmet fish feed and postmodern poetry.', 3);
INSERT INTO ITEM(id, itemId, name, description, quantity) VALUES (4,
'lion', 'lion', 'Big cat with fancy mane. Loves playing the tag and
cuddling with other animals and people.', 9);
```

After all that is finally done, we should be able to see our application working. Let's try it now:

```
2018-03-08 01:46:49,840 INFO  [org.jboss.weld.Version] (MSC service thread 1-3) WELD-000900: 2.4.3 (Final)
2018-03-08 01:46:49,884 INFO  [org.wildfly.extension.undertow] (MSC service thread 1-5) WFLYUT0018: Host default-host starting
2018-03-08 01:46:49,891 INFO  [org.jboss.as.connector.deployers.jdbc] (MSC service thread 1-4) WFLYJCA0018: Started Driver service with driver-name
2018-03-08 01:46:49,977 ERROR [org.jboss.as.controller.management-operation] (main) WFLYCTL0013: Operation ("add") failed - address: {("deployment"
were unable to start due to one or more indirect dependencies not being available." => {
    "Services that were unable to start:" => [
        "jboss.deployment.unit.\"catalog-service-1.0.war\".CdiValidatorFactoryService",
        "jboss.deployment.unit.\"catalog-service-1.0.war\".WeldStartService",
        "jboss.deployment.unit.\"catalog-service-1.0.war\".component.\"javax.servlet.jsp.jstl.tlv.PermittedTaglibsTLV\".START",
        "jboss.deployment.unit.\"catalog-service-1.0.war\".component.\"javax.servlet.jsp.jstl.tlv.PermittedTaglibsTLV\".WeldInstantiator",
        "jboss.deployment.unit.\"catalog-service-1.0.war\".component.\"javax.servlet.jsp.jstl.tlv.ScriptFreeTLV\".START",
        "jboss.deployment.unit.\"catalog-service-1.0.war\".component.\"javax.servlet.jsp.jstl.tlv.ScriptFreeTLV\".WeldInstantiator",
        "jboss.deployment.unit.\"catalog-service-1.0.war\".component.\"org.jboss.weld.servlet.WeldInitialListener\".START",
        "jboss.deployment.unit.\"catalog-service-1.0.war\".component.\"org.jboss.weld.servlet.WeldInitialListener\".WeldInstantiator",
        "jboss.deployment.unit.\"catalog-service-1.0.war\".component.\"org.jboss.weld.servlet.WeldTerminalListener\".START",
        "jboss.deployment.unit.\"catalog-service-1.0.war\".component.\"org.jboss.weld.servlet.WeldTerminalListener\".WeldInstantiator",
        "jboss.deployment.unit.\"catalog-service-1.0.war\".deploymentCompleteService",
        "jboss.deployment.unit.\"catalog-service-1.0.war\".jndiDependencyService",
        "jboss.naming.context.java.module.\"catalog-service-1.0\".\"catalog-service-1.0\".DefaultDataSource",
        "jboss.persistenceunit.\"catalog-service-1.0.war#CatalogPU\"",
        "jboss.persistenceunit.\"catalog-service-1.0.war#CatalogPU\".__FIRST_PHASE__",
        "jboss.undertow.deployment.default-server.default-host./",
        "jboss.undertow.deployment.default-server.default-host./.UndertowDeploymentInfoService"
    ],
    "Services that may be the cause:" => ["jboss.jdbc-driver.h2"]
}}
```

Oops! Instead of the browser page with a message, an awful red log appears. What went wrong? Let's take a look at the first read message: `"WFLYJCA0041: Failed to load module for driver [com.h2database.h2]"`. True, as this is a custom driver module, we have to add it to our application manually. How are we able to do that? That is simple too.

To add an additional custom module to our application, we have to add it to the `resources` directory of our application:

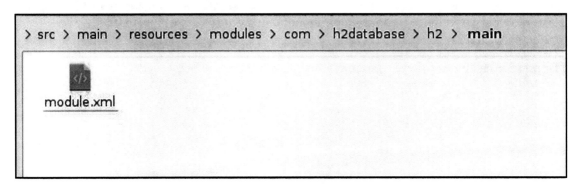

As shown in the preceding screenshot, the `modules` directory has to be placed inside the Maven's `resources` directory inside our application, and the directory structure has to match the module name. Let's look at the module descriptor:

```xml
<?xml version="1.0" encoding="UTF-8"?>
<!-- 1 -->
<module xmlns="urn:jboss:module:1.3" name="com.h2database.h2">

  <resources>
    <!-- 2 -->
    <artifact name="com.h2database:h2:1.4.187"/>
  </resources>
  <!-- 3 -->
  <dependencies>
    <module name="javax.api"/>
    <module name="javax.transaction.api"/>
    <module name="javax.servlet.api" optional="true"/>
  </dependencies>
</module>
```

To recall, this is the same kind of descriptor that we presented in Chapter 2, *Getting Familiar with WildFly Swarm*, where we described the concept of modular classloading. In the preceding file, we are creating a module with the `"com.h2database.h2"` name (1), specifying that the only resource is the `h2` database artifact. Note that we are referencing the artifact using Maven coordinates. Finally, we have to specify all the module dependencies (3).

Let's build and run the application again. We are indeed able to look up our pets now:

We are indeed, able to search pets by `id` now.

Let's continue with the `Swarm` class usage. The next thing that we will look at is its `deploy` method.

Modifying your archive

In our previous examples, each time we created the `Swarm` instance and applied some configuration on top of it, we used the no-argument `deploy` method. This method takes the archive generated by the standard Maven build and deploys it on the previously configured container. This is not the only version of the `deploy` method, though. You are able to create your own archive (or archives) and deploy them to the Swarm container. How? It is possible using the `ShrinkWrap` API.

The ShrinkWrap API

If you have ever worked with WildFly AS, and, especially, its testing framework Arquillian, you are probably also familiar with the `ShrinkWrap` API, which is used to build application archives before they are deployed in the test environment. However, if you have never used it, don't worry—the API is very simple and straightforward.

The central class in the API is the `org.jboss.shrinkwrap.api.Archive` instance. It is an abstract class that represents the archive. The concrete implementations that interest us the most are `org.jboss.shrinkwrap.api.spec.JavaArchive` and `org.jboss.shrinkwrap.api.spec.WebArchive` that represent JARs and WARs as you probably have guessed. The API is simple; it contains a bunch of methods that allow you to add resources to the archive. Let's see its operation in practice.

For the sake of this example, let's return to the first CatalogService version, which contained only the jaxrs resource and application.

 Examples reference: chapter4/catalog-service-shrinkwrap

To see the ShrinkWrap in action, we have to modify the pom.xml file:

```
(...)

    <dependencies>
        <dependency>
            <groupId>org.jboss.spec.javax.ws.rs</groupId>
            <artifactId>jboss-jaxrs-api_2.0_spec</artifactId>
            <scope>provided</scope>
        </dependency>
        <!-- 1 -->
        <dependency>
            <groupId>org.wildfly.swarm</groupId>
            <artifactId>jaxrs</artifactId>
            <version>${version.wildfly.swarm}</version>
        </dependency>
    </dependencies>

    <build>
        <plugins>
            <plugin>
                <artifactId>maven-war-plugin</artifactId>
                <version>${version.war.plugin}</version>
                <configuration>
                    <failOnMissingWebXml>false</failOnMissingWebXml>
                </configuration>
            </plugin>
            <plugin>
                <groupId>org.wildfly.swarm</groupId>
                <artifactId>wildfly-swarm-plugin</artifactId>
                <version>${version.wildfly.swarm}</version>
                <!-- 2 -->
                <configuration>
<mainClass>org.packt.swarm.petstore.catalog.Main</mainClass>
                </configuration>
                <executions>
                    <execution>
                        <goals>
                            <goal>package</goal>
```

```
            </goals>
          </execution>
        </executions>
      </plugin>
    </plugins>
  </build>

(...)
```

As we are providing our own `main`, we have to explicitly add the dependency on the `jaxrs` fraction (1). We also have to add the method to the Swarm plugin configuration (2).

Let's look at the `ShrinkWrap` API usage in the `org.packt.swarm.petstore.Main` class:

```
package org.packt.swarm.petstore.catalog;

import org.jboss.shrinkwrap.api.ShrinkWrap;
import org.wildfly.swarm.Swarm;
import org.wildfly.swarm.jaxrs.JAXRSArchive;

public class Main {

    public static void main(String[] args) throws Exception {

        Swarm swarm = new Swarm();
        swarm.start();

        //1
        JAXRSArchive deployment = ShrinkWrap.create(JAXRSArchive.class,
"deployment.war");
        //2
        deployment.addClasses(CatalogApplication.class,
CatalogResource.class, Item.class);
        swarm.deploy(deployment);
    }
}
```

We created the web archive (1), added the classes that our example consists of (2), and deployed them on the created container (3). As a result, we have manually done the same thing that Swarm does for us automatically.

We have used the addClass method to add created classes to the archive. In a similar way, you are able to use other ShrinkWrap API methods.

The org.jboss.shrinkwrap.api.spec.JavaArchive class apart from the native archive methods (add and addDirectory)) contains the methods that make it easy to work with classes (addClass and addPackage), resources (addResource), and manifests (setManifest and addManifestResource).

The org.jboss.shrinkwrap.api.spec.WebArchive class additionally adds web resource methods (addWebResource and setWebXML). As in the preceding example, using those methods is usually straightforward, but in the case of any doubts, you can take advantage of the ShrinkWrap Java API.

Obtaining the default archive

Isn't ShrinkWrap too tedious to be useful in any real-life circumstances? After all, we don't want to manually add all classes and resources from our application to the archive. You don't have to worry about it—you will be able to obtain default deployment from the Swarm instance:

```
package org.packt.swarm.petstore.catalog;

import org.jboss.shrinkwrap.api.Archive;
import org.wildfly.swarm.Swarm;

public class Main {

  public static void main(String[] args) throws Exception {

  Swarm swarm = new Swarm();
  swarm.start();

  //1
  Archive<?> deployment = swarm.createDefaultDeployment();
  swarm.deploy(deployment);

  }

}
```

As you see in the preceding example, we were able to obtain the default deployment by invoking the createDefaultDeployment() method. After we have it, we can only additional needed resources to it.

Swarm ShrinkWrap extensions

Swarm adds its own classes to complement the `ShripWrap` API. Let's introduce them.

JARArchive

The `org.wildfly.swarm.spi.api.JARArchive` is an alternative to the `JavaArchive`. Apart from all functions provided by it, the `JARArchive` adds an API to easily add modules, Maven dependencies, and service provider implementations.

WARArchive

As the `WebArchive` adds a functionality on top of `JavaArchive`, the `WARArchive` adds new features on top of the `JARArchive`. Apart from an interface that allows working with web resources, it adds the possibility to easily add the static web content. Let's look at this for an example.

As usual, we need the `pom.xml`:

```
(...)

    <!-- 1 -->
    <dependencies>
        <dependency>
            <groupId>org.wildfly.swarm</groupId>
            <artifactId>undertow</artifactId>
            <version>${version.wildfly.swarm}</version>
        </dependency>
    </dependencies>

(...)
```

As we are using our own `main`, we will need to add an `undertow` fraction dependency (1) and configure the `main` method (2).

Our static content will be a simple **Hello World** page:

```
<html>
<body>
<h1>Hello World!</h1>
</body>
</html>
```

We will add this class to the `webpage` directory inside our application's resources:

The `main` class looks like this:

```
package org.packt.swarm.petstore.catalog;

import org.jboss.shrinkwrap.api.ShrinkWrap;
import org.wildfly.swarm.Swarm;
import org.wildfly.swarm.undertow.WARArchive;

public class Main {

    public static void main(String[] args) throws Exception {

        Swarm swarm = new Swarm();

        //1
        WARArchive deployment = ShrinkWrap.create(WARArchive.class);
        //2
        deployment.staticContent("webpage");

        swarm.start().deploy(deployment);

    }
}
```

We have created the `WARArchive` and invoked the `staticContent` method. When we open the web browser, we will see the **Hello World** page:

What has happened? The static content method has copied all non-Java files from the `webpage` directory (one file in our example) to the created archive so that they can be seen by `undertow`.

JAXRSArchive

The last type of Swarm archive that we want to look at right now is the `org.wildfly.swarm.JAXRSArchive`. This archive adds the ability to create a default JAX-RS application with the application path set to `"/"`. Till now, we have been doing this manually in all our examples. With the JAX-RS Archive, this class will be added automatically.

XML configuration

Although Java API is convenient, this is not the only option that we have. If you are familiar with the WildFly XML configuration, or if you are migrating your application to Swarm and have a working XML file, you don't have to translate it to Java API as you can use it directly.

Examples reference: `chapter4/catalog-service-xmlconfig`

Let's return to our database example. You may configure the datasource using XML. In such a case, the XML configuration will look like this:

```xml
<subsystem xmlns="urn:jboss:domain:datasources:4.0">
    <datasources>
        <drivers>
            <driver name="h2" module="com.h2database.h2">
                <driver-class>org.h2.Driver</driver-class>
                <xa-datasource-class>org.h2.jdbcx.JdbcDataSource</xa-
datasource-class>
            </driver>
        </drivers>
        <datasource jndi-name="java:jboss/datasources/CatalogDS" pool-
name="CatalogDS" enabled="true" use-java-context="true">
            <connection-
url>jdbc:h2:mem:test;DB_CLOSE_DELAY=-1;DB_CLOSE_ON_EXIT=FALSE</connection-
url>
            <driver>h2</driver>
        </datasource>
        <datasource jndi-name="java:jboss/datasources/ExampleDS" pool-
name="ExampleDS" enabled="true" use-java-context="true">
            <connection-
url>jdbc:h2:mem:test;DB_CLOSE_DELAY=-1;DB_CLOSE_ON_EXIT=FALSE</connection-
url>
            <driver>h2</driver>
            <security>
                <user-name>sa</user-name>
                <password>sa</password>
            </security>
        </datasource>
    </datasources>
</subsystem>
```

We have to add this configuration file to the `resources` directory:

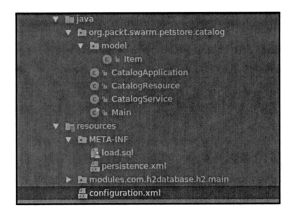

Finally, we also have to tell Swarm to use the configuration file. The following is the modified `Main` class:

```
package org.packt.swarm.petstore.catalog;

import org.jboss.shrinkwrap.api.Archive;
import org.wildfly.swarm.Swarm;
import org.wildfly.swarm.datasources.DatasourcesFraction;
import org.wildfly.swarm.jaxrs.JAXRSArchive;
import org.wildfly.swarm.undertow.UndertowFraction;
import org.wildfly.swarm.undertow.WARArchive;

import java.net.URL;

public class Main {

    public static void main(String[] args) throws Exception {

        Swarm swarm = new Swarm();

        //1
        ClassLoader cl = Main.class.getClassLoader();
        URL xmlConfig = cl.getResource("datasources.xml");

        //2
        swarm.withXmlConfig(xmlConfig);

        swarm.start().deploy();

    }
```

We have obtained the classloader to be able to locate the configuration file(1). After reading the file, we instructed Swarm to use the configuration from it (2).

However, we have used the whole configuration file—will Swarm use all the subsystems now? The answer is no; only the fractions, whose dependencies have been specified will be added to the container. Swarm, given the XML file, will read only the configuration of those subsystems whose fractions constitute it. You are also able to provide a file with only those subsystems that you want to configure using XML.

YAML configuration

Another way in which you can provide Swarm configuration is YAML data serialization language.

Once more, let's start with the port-change example. We will start again with JAX-RS example and modify it to use the YAML configuration.

First, let's create the HTTP-`port.yml` configuration file inside the `resources` directory:

```
swarm:
  http:
    port: 12345
```

The nested properties are translated to flat properties by Swarm. So, the property specified by the preceding file is translated to `swarm.http.port`, which we know well already.

To use the following configuration, we have to modify our `Main` class:

```
package org.packt.swarm.petstore.catalog;

import org.wildfly.swarm.Swarm;

import java.net.URL;

public class Main {

    public static void main(String[] args) throws Exception {

        Swarm swarm = new Swarm();

        //1
        ClassLoader cl = Main.class.getClassLoader();
        URL yamlConfig = cl.getResource("http-port.yml");
```

```
//2
swarm.withConfig(yamlConfig);

swarm.start().deploy();
    }
}
```

After obtaining the configuration from the `classpath` (1), we informed Swarm to use it using the `withConfig` method. That's it; now, Swarm will use the `12345` port.

Project stages

The strength of the YAML configuration is its ability to provide different groups properties for different project stages. Again, let's take a look at the example first.

The new configuration file looks like this:

```
swarm:
  http:
    port: 8080
---
project:
    stage: test
swarm:
    http:
        port: 12345
---
project:
    stage: QA
swarm:
    http:
        port: 12346
```

The different parts of the file gather the configuration for different project stages. The first group is the default configuration. It is used when no stage name is provided. The other two specify the configurations for test and QA stages. However, how do you know the stage in which the application currently runs? You have to provide the `swarm.project.stage` property. So, consider that, for example, we run the preceding example with the following command:

```
mvn wildfly-swarm:run -Dswarm.project.stage=QA
```

Then, we will be able to access our application on the `12346` port.

As you will have noticed in the preceding code, the YAML configuration makes it easy to create the configuration for different environments and choose what group of properties should be used using a simple command-line argument.

YAML database configuration

As an another YAML config example, we are going to show you how to configure the datasources with the YAML configuration file. Let's take a look:

 Examples reference: `chapter 4/catalog-service-database-ymlconfig`

The example is very similar to the XML configuration example. We have to exchange the configuration file for its YAML equivalent:

```
swarm:
  datasources:
    data-sources:
      CatalogDS:
        driver-name: h2
        connection-url:
jdbc:h2:mem:test;DB_CLOSE_DELAY=-1;DB_CLOSE_ON_EXIT=FALSE
        user-name: sa
        password: sa
    jdbc-drivers:
        h2:
          driver-class-name: org.h2.Driver
          xa-datasource-name: org.h2.jdbcx.JdbcDataSource
          driver-module-name: com.h2database.h2
```

And also need to make the `Main` class use it (1):

```
package org.packt.swarm.petstore.catalog;

import org.wildfly.swarm.Swarm;

import java.net.URL;

public class Main {

    public static void main(String[] args) throws Exception {
        Swarm swarm = new Swarm();
```

```
            //1
            ClassLoader cl = Main.class.getClassLoader();
            URL ymlConfig = cl.getResource("datasources.yml");

            swarm.withConfig(ymlConfig);

            swarm.start().deploy();
        }
    }
```

We are going to use such configurations a lot in the examples throughout the book.

Mixing the configurations

Now, what about mixing configurations? Are you allowed to do this? Yup. Let's look at the following code:

```
package org.packt.swarm.petstore.catalog;

import org.jboss.shrinkwrap.api.Archive;
import org.wildfly.swarm.Swarm;
import org.wildfly.swarm.datasources.DatasourcesFraction;
import org.wildfly.swarm.undertow.UndertowFraction;

public class Main {

 public static void main(String[] args) throws Exception {
 Swarm swarm = new Swarm();

 //1
 ClassLoader cl = Main.class.getClassLoader();
 URL xmlConfig = cl.getResource("standalone.xml");
 swarm.withXMLFile(xmlFile);

 //2
 UndertowFraction undertowFraction = new UndertowFraction();
 undertowFraction.applyDefaults();
 undertowFraction.httpPort(12345);
 swarm.fraction(undertowFraction);

 //3
 Archive<?> deployment = swarm.createDefaultDeployment();
 deployment.addModule("com.h2database.h2");

 //4
```

```
swarm.start().deploy();
    }

}
```

It is another variation of our database example, and you already know what is happening in the whole code. Just to recall, we loaded the configuration file and informed Swarm to use it (1), created the `UndertowFraction` and configured it to use the `12345` port (2), added the driver module to the application (3), and, finally, started the application and deployed the created archive on it (4).

What would be the result of such code? As you probably have guessed, after running the application, we will be able to see the random messages on `localhost:12345/hello`.

Note that you are able to mix XML and Java API configurations. Can you use the properties too? Sure. Let's add `swarm.http.port` with the `12346` port to the command line, and we will be able to see our messages on the address. Yeah, we have a conflict here. Is this an error? It is not an error. Swarm attaches different priorities to different configuration methods. The precedence is as follows:

1. Java API overrides the configuration specified by XML
2. YAML overrides the configuration specified by Java API
3. Finally, the system properties override the YAML configuration
4. As a result, in our last example, we will see our messages on the `12346` port

Summary

In this chapter, you learned how to configure services created using Swarm. You learned how to modify the Swarm behavior using the system properties, provide your own `main` method and use it to provide the Swarm configuration using either Java API or XML, and, finally, how to modify the content of the deployed application.

After the three initial chapters, you are now able to use WildFly Swarm to build microservices. In the next chapters, you will learn OpenShift so you are able to deploy your services in the cloud.

Further reading

```
http://wildfly-swarm.io/documentation/
```

Testing Your Services with Arquillian

5

In this chapter, you will learn how to test your microservices. For this purpose, we will use Arquillian, a test framework designed to test software components using their dedicated runtime, instead of creating mock-based unit tests. This is the framework developer to work seamlessly WildFly Swarm and, effectively, a framework of choice for it.

We will introduce Arquillian and present the purpose of the project and its main features. Later, you will learn how to develop, write, and configure tests for your services based on practical examples.

Introducing Arquillian

We all know the benefits of unit testing. They are simple and run immediately. They isolate the components of your application and allow you to test them one by one, providing the coverage of each component's usage scenarios.

Unfortunately, unit tests have their shortcomings too. When you cover your application with unit tests, they will confirm that each component of your application works correctly. Obviously, based only on that information, you cannot deduce that your whole application works correctly—that is a reason to have integration tests. You have to test your components inside the environment in which they will operate to ensure that the application works correctly as a whole.

The problem with integration tests so far has been that they tend to be complicated to configure and took a long time to execute. Here is where Arquillian steps in. The aim of the project is to make integration tests as fast and simple to configure as unit tests.

As you may recall, in `Chapter 2`, *Getting Familiar with WildFly Swarm*, we emphasized how fast modern runtimes are. Arquillian takes advantage of that and lets you easily configure the tests that run on the same runtime your application will run. If, for example, you are developing a Java EE application, you can configure Arquillian to run the test on the application server of your choice. Since modern applications servers are very fast, the test will run immediately. On the other hand, you will be able to test your application in its real environment with all its dependencies.

In our case, a runtime for each service is assembled by WildFly Swarm (as described in `Chapter 3`, *Right-Sizing Your Applications*). Arquillian allows you to configure the tests for such cases too. Let's find out how.

Testing Swarm microservices with Arquillian

In this section, you will learn how Arquillian can be used to test microservices created with Swarm. As you learned in previous chapters, Swarm builds a runtime containing only fractions needed by a given service, starts it, and then deploys an archive on it, creating the microservice.

Arquillian, as we have just learned, tests an application on its dedicated runtime. It starts the runtime, deploys the tested code on it, and performs the test. Let's configure such a test for our JAX-RS and the CDI catalog service example, and explain what we are doing step by step.

 For examples: refer to `chapter 5/catalog-service-simple-test`.

First of all, we have to provide all the necessary dependencies:

```
(...)

    <dependencyManagement>
        <dependencies>
            <!-- 1 -->
            <dependency>
                <groupId>org.jboss.arquillian</groupId>
                <artifactId>arquillian-bom</artifactId>
                <version>${version.arquillian}</version>
                <type>pom</type>
                <scope>import</scope>
```

```xml
            </dependency>
        </dependencies>
    </dependencyManagement>

    <dependencies>
        <dependency>
            <groupId>org.wildfly.swarm</groupId>
            <artifactId>jaxrs</artifactId>
            <version>${version.wildfly.swarm}</version>
        </dependency>
        <dependency>
            <groupId>org.wildfly.swarm</groupId>
            <artifactId>cdi</artifactId>
            <version>${version.wildfly.swarm}</version>
        </dependency>
        <!-- 2 -->
        <dependency>
            <groupId>junit</groupId>
            <artifactId>junit</artifactId>
            <version>${version.junit}</version>
            <scope>test</scope>
        </dependency>
        <!-- 3 -->
        <dependency>
            <groupId>org.jboss.arquillian.junit</groupId>
            <artifactId>arquillian-junit-container</artifactId>
            <scope>test</scope>
        </dependency>
        <!-- 4 -->
        <dependency>
            <groupId>org.wildfly.swarm</groupId>
            <artifactId>arquillian</artifactId>
            <version>${version.wildfly.swarm}</version>
            <scope>test</scope>
        </dependency>

    </dependencies>

(...)

</project>
```

1. Firstly, we added Arquillian to dependencyManagement (1).

2. Secondly, Arquillian can be integrated with various testing libraries. As we are going to use JUnit, we have to provide the dependency to it (2).

3. To run the Arquillian test with JUnit, we have to provide JUnit integration artifact (3).

4. Thirdly, we have to tell Arquillian which runtime to use—we are doing this by providing a dependency to an adapter library. In our case, this obviously is a Swarm adapter (3).

Now we are ready to take a look at the code. To recall, the service in this example contains only one item, which is added manually:

```java
package org.packt.swarm.petstore.catalog;

import org.packt.swarm.petstore.catalog.model.Item;

import javax.enterprise.context.ApplicationScoped;
import java.util.HashMap;
import java.util.Map;

@ApplicationScoped
public class CatalogService {

    private Map<String, Item> catalog = new HashMap<>();

    public CatalogService(){
        Item turtle = new Item();
        turtle.setItemId("turtle");
        turtle.setName("turtle");
        turtle.setQuantity(5);
        turtle.setDescription("Slow, friendly reptile. Let your busy self
see how it spends 100 years of his life laying on sand and swimming.");
        catalog.put("turtle", turtle);
    }

    public Item searchById(String itemId){
        return catalog.get(itemId);
    }

}
```

Now it is time to write a `test` class. An Arquillian-based test runs in the following way: Arquillian looks for the static method annotated with the `org.jboss.arquillian.container.test.api.Deployment` annotation. The method has to return the `ShrinkWrap` archive.

Arquillian will start the container and deploy the returned archive on it. After that, the methods are annotated with `org.junit`. A test runs inside the container. Let's look at all this in our sample test:

```
package org.packt.swarm.petstore.catalog;

import org.jboss.arquillian.container.test.api.Deployment;
import org.jboss.arquillian.junit.Arquillian;
import org.jboss.shrinkwrap.api.ShrinkWrap;
import org.jboss.shrinkwrap.api.asset.EmptyAsset;
import org.jboss.shrinkwrap.api.spec.JavaArchive;
import org.junit.Assert;
import org.junit.Test;
import org.junit.runner.RunWith;
import org.packt.swarm.petstore.catalog.model.Item;

import javax.inject.Inject;

//1
@RunWith(Arquillian.class)
public class CatalogServiceTest {

    //2
    @Deployment
    public static JavaArchive createDeployment() {
        return ShrinkWrap.create(JavaArchive.class)
                .addClasses(Item.class,CatalogService.class)
                .addAsManifestResource(EmptyAsset.INSTANCE, "beans.xml");
    }

    //3
    @Inject
    CatalogService catalogService;

    //4
    @Test
    public void testSearchById() {
Assert.assertEquals(catalogService.searchById("turtle").getName(),"turtle")
;
    }
}
```

In the beginning, we told JUnit to run the test using Arquillian test controller. To do that, we annotated the test with the @RunWith annotation, specifying Arquillian.class as the test runner (1).

The createDeployment (2) method, as its name suggests, is responsible for creating the deployment archive, which will be deployed on the configured container. To inform Arquillian about it, we have to annotate this method with the @Deployment annotation. The method is static and returns the ShrinkWrap archive. As the test method is being run inside the container, we are able to inject its resources. In our example, we have to inject the CatalogService class that we are going to test (3) and the Item class on which it depends.

Finally, the Test method checks whether the searchById method works correctly (4).

Let's run the test now:

```
mvn clean wildfly-swarm:run
```

You will note that the test has been deployed inside the Swarm container:

```
T E S T S
-------------------------------------------------------
Running org.packt.swarm.petstore.catalog.CatalogServiceTest
Resolving 0 out of 541 artifacts
Sat Mar 10 17:36:28 CET 2018 INFO [org.wildfly.swarm.bootstrap] (main) Dependencies not bundled;
2018-03-10 17:36:31,633 INFO  [org.wildfly.swarm] (main) WFSWARM0013: Installed fraction:
2018-03-10 17:36:31,637 INFO  [org.wildfly.swarm] (main) WFSWARM0013: Installed fraction:
2018-03-10 17:36:31,638 INFO  [org.wildfly.swarm] (main) WFSWARM0013: Installed fraction:
2018-03-10 17:36:31,638 INFO  [org.wildfly.swarm] (main) WFSWARM0013: Installed fraction:
2018-03-10 17:36:31,638 INFO  [org.wildfly.swarm] (main) WFSWARM0013: Installed fraction:
2018-03-10 17:36:31,639 INFO  [org.wildfly.swarm] (main) WFSWARM0013: Installed fraction:
2018-03-10 17:36:31,639 INFO  [org.wildfly.swarm] (main) WFSWARM0013: Installed fraction:
2018-03-10 17:36:31,639 INFO  [org.wildfly.swarm] (main) WFSWARM0013: Installed fraction:
2018-03-10 17:36:33,206 INFO  [org.jboss.msc] (main) JBoss MSC version 1.2.7.SP1
2018-03-10 17:36:33,299 INFO  [org.jboss.as] (MSC service thread 1-7) WFLYSRV0049: WildFly Swarm
2018-03-10 17:36:33,332 INFO  [org.wildfly.swarm] (MSC service thread 1-7) WFSWARM0019: Install
2018-03-10 17:36:33,532 INFO  [org.wildfly.swarm.arquillian.daemon.server.Server] (MSC service t
2018-03-10 17:36:33,945 INFO  [org.wildfly.security] (ServerService Thread Pool -- 3) ELY00001:
2018-03-10 17:36:33,980 INFO  [org.jboss.as.naming] (ServerService Thread Pool -- 15) WFLYNAM000
```

It finishes successfully:

```
2018-03-10 17:36:36,307 INFO  [stdout] (MSC service thread 1-1) [Server] Serv
2018-03-10 17:36:36,307 INFO  [null] (MSC service thread 1-1) Server shutdown
2018-03-10 17:36:36,337 INFO  [org.jboss.as.server.deployment] (MSC service t
2018-03-10 17:36:36,347 INFO  [org.jboss.as] (MSC service thread 1-8) WFLYSRV
2018-03-10 17:36:36,370 INFO  [org.jboss.weld.Bootstrap] (pool-1-thread-1) WE

Tests run: 1, Failures: 0, Errors: 0, Skipped: 0, Time elapsed: 12.054 sec

Results :

Tests run: 1, Failures: 0, Errors: 0, Skipped: 0

[INFO]
[INFO] --- maven-war-plugin:2.1.1:war (default-war) @ catalog-service ---
[INFO] Packaging webapp
[INFO] Assembling webapp [catalog-service] in [/home/tomek/książka/swarm-exam
[INFO] Processing war project
```

Finally, the Swarm microservice starts (because we used the `wildfly-swarm:run`
command):

```
Resolving 52 out of 266 artifacts
[INFO] Repackaging .war: /home/tomek/książka/swarm-examples/example-catalog-service/target/cat
[INFO] Repackaged .war: /home/tomek/książka/swarm-examples/example-catalog-service/target/cata
[INFO]
[INFO] <<< wildfly-swarm-plugin:2018.3.0:run (default-cli) < package @ catalog-service <<<
[INFO]
[INFO] --- wildfly-swarm-plugin:2018.3.0:run (default-cli) @ catalog-service ---
[INFO] Starting .war
Sat Mar 10 17:36:41 CET 2018 INFO [org.wildfly.swarm.bootstrap] (main) Dependencies not bundle
2018-03-10 17:36:43,373 INFO  [org.wildfly.swarm] (main) WFSWARM0013: Installed fraction:
2018-03-10 17:36:43,378 INFO  [org.wildfly.swarm] (main) WFSWARM0013: Installed fraction:
2018-03-10 17:36:43,378 INFO  [org.wildfly.swarm] (main) WFSWARM0013: Installed fraction:
2018-03-10 17:36:43,378 INFO  [org.wildfly.swarm] (main) WFSWARM0013: Installed fraction:
2018-03-10 17:36:43,378 INFO  [org.wildfly.swarm] (main) WFSWARM0013: Installed fraction:
2018-03-10 17:36:43,379 INFO  [org.wildfly.swarm] (main) WFSWARM0013: Installed fraction:
2018-03-10 17:36:43,379 INFO  [org.wildfly.swarm] (main) WFSWARM0013: Installed fraction:
2018-03-10 17:36:43,379 INFO  [org.wildfly.swarm] (main) WFSWARM0013: Installed fraction:
```

Note that Swarm, as in examples from the previous chapters, used the when-missing
discovery mechanism and created the container with all the necessary fractions. That
container was used for both testing and running the resulting microservices.

As you could notice in the preceding screenshot, the only file that we changed was the pom.xml file, so the switch from AS to Swarm was again very simple. However, this had drawbacks too: not changing the CatalogTest class meant that we were again creating the archive manually—Swarm can do it for us when the service is created so can't it create the deployment test too? It can—let's learn how.

The default deployment

As we have just hinted, Swarm can create the default test deployment.

For example, refer to chapter 5/catalog-service-test-default-deployment.

We will modify the Test class so that the archive is created automatically:

```
package org.packt.swarm.petstore.catalog;

import org.jboss.arquillian.junit.Arquillian;
import org.junit.Assert;
import org.junit.Test;
import org.junit.runner.RunWith;
import org.wildfly.swarm.arquillian.DefaultDeployment;

import javax.inject.Inject;


@RunWith(Arquillian.class)
//1
@DefaultDeployment
public class CatalogServiceTest {

    @Inject
    CatalogService catalogService;

    @Test
    public void testSearchById() {
Assert.assertEquals(catalogService.searchById("turtle").getName(),"turtle")
;
    }
}
```

In order to tell Swarm to create the test deployment automatically, we have to annotate the class with the `org.wildfly.swarm.arquillian.DefaultDeployment` annotation (1). That's just it. If you run the test now, you will see the same result as in the preceding paragraph. Note that we didn't use the `@Deployment` annotated static method as we did in the preceding example.

Swarm configuration

In the preceding chapter, we showed you how to modify the Swarm configuration. The example that we used to present that was a database configuration. In this section, we will show you how to provide analogous configuration for a Swarm test using the same example.

For examples, refer to `chapter 5/catalog-service-database-test`.

If you would like to create the Swarm container manually, you have to implement the static method annotated with the `org.wildfly.swarm.arquillian.CreateSwarm` annotation and return the instance of the `org.wildfly.swarm.Swarm` class from it. As you probably recall, we have already created a lot of Swarm containers inside the `main` functions that we created in `Chapter 4`, *Tuning the Configuration of Your Services*. Swarm-creating methods that we will use in the tests work the same way. Let's take a look at the code:

```
package org.packt.swarm.petstore.catalog;

import org.jboss.arquillian.container.test.api.Deployment;
import org.jboss.arquillian.junit.Arquillian;
import org.jboss.shrinkwrap.api.ShrinkWrap;
import org.jboss.shrinkwrap.api.asset.EmptyAsset;
import org.jboss.shrinkwrap.api.spec.JavaArchive;
import org.junit.Assert;
import org.junit.Test;
import org.junit.runner.RunWith;
import org.packt.swarm.petstore.catalog.model.Item;
import org.wildfly.swarm.Swarm;
import org.wildfly.swarm.arquillian.CreateSwarm;

import javax.inject.Inject;
import java.net.URL;

//1
```

```
@RunWith(Arquillian.class)
public class CatalogServiceTest {

    @Deployment
    public static JavaArchive createDeployment() {
        return ShrinkWrap.create(JavaArchive.class)
                .addClasses(Item.class, CatalogService.class)
                //1
                .addAsResource("datasources.yml")
                .addAsResource("META-INF/persistence.xml")
                .addAsResource("META-INF/load.sql")
                .addAsManifestResource(EmptyAsset.INSTANCE, "beans.xml");
    }

    //2
    @CreateSwarm
    public static Swarm createSwarm() throws Exception {
        Swarm swarm = new Swarm();
        //3
        ClassLoader cl = CatalogServiceTest.class.getClassLoader();
        URL dataSourcesConfig = cl.getResource("datasources.yml");
        //4
        swarm.withConfig(dataSourcesConfig);
        return swarm;
    }

    //4
    @Inject
    CatalogService catalogService;

    //5
    @Test
    public void testSearchById() {
Assert.assertEquals(catalogService.searchById("turtle").getName(),"turtle")
;
    }
}
```

In the beginning, we created the deployment with all the necessary classes and configurations.

We have to add the datasource configuration, the persistence configuration, and the load file (1) so that they can be read from within the test.

The key part is the `createSwarm` method (2) mentioned previously. It creates the Swarm instance, reads the datasources configuration (3), and configures Swarm with it (4).

When the container and deployment are ready, we can start writing the test logic. We start by injecting the `CatalogService` to the test (4). Recall that this test runs inside the Swarm container, and as a result, the service can be injected into it. Finally, to ensure that our service indeed works correctly, we check whether the returned data is correct (5).
If you run the test now, you will see that it passes correctly.
However, currently, we are creating the microservices without any endpoints and testing them from inside the container. That's OK, but we would also like to test the whole microservice, using its external interface. Let's take a look at how to do it.

Testing from a standalone client

This time, we would like to test the application from a standalone client. Let's learn how to do it.

 For examples, refer to `chapter 5/catalog-service-database-test-standalone`.

First of all, we have to add a bunch of dependencies to the `pom.xml` file:

```
(...)

<dependencies>
(...)
    <dependency>
        <groupId>org.wildfly.swarm</groupId>
        <artifactId>arquillian</artifactId>
        <version>${version.wildfly.swarm}</version>
        <scope>test</scope>
    </dependency>

    <!-- 1 -->
    <dependency>
        <groupId>org.jboss.resteasy</groupId>
        <artifactId>resteasy-client</artifactId>
        <version>${resteasy.version}</version>
        <scope>test</scope>
    </dependency>

    <!-- 2 -->
```

```
<dependency>
    <groupId>org.jboss.resteasy</groupId>
    <artifactId>resteasy-jackson-provider</artifactId>
    <version>${resteasy.version}</version>
    <scope>test</scope>
</dependency>

</dependencies>
(...)
```

We have to add a dependency to the JAX-RS client that we will use to make REST invocations on our service. As we will use the `resteasy` implementation, we will add its client (1). We would also need a library to parse the JSON response, hence the `resteasy-jackson-provider` is added (2).

Let's take a look at the code of the test that does it:

```
package org.packt.swarm.petstore.catalog;

import org.jboss.arquillian.container.test.api.Deployment;
import org.jboss.arquillian.container.test.api.RunAsClient;
import org.jboss.arquillian.junit.Arquillian;
import org.jboss.arquillian.test.api.ArquillianResource;
import org.jboss.shrinkwrap.api.ShrinkWrap;
import org.jboss.shrinkwrap.api.asset.EmptyAsset;
import org.jboss.shrinkwrap.api.spec.WebArchive;
import org.junit.Assert;
import org.junit.BeforeClass;
import org.junit.Test;
import org.junit.runner.RunWith;
import org.packt.swarm.petstore.catalog.model.Item;
import org.wildfly.swarm.Swarm;
import org.wildfly.swarm.arquillian.CreateSwarm;

import javax.ws.rs.client.Client;
import javax.ws.rs.client.ClientBuilder;
import javax.ws.rs.client.WebTarget;
import java.net.URL;

@RunWith(Arquillian.class)
public class CatalogServiceTest {

    @Deployment
    public static WebArchive createDeployment() {
        return ShrinkWrap.create(WebArchive.class)
                //1
                .addClasses(Item.class, CatalogService.class,
```

```
CatalogResource.class, CatalogApplication.class)
                .addAsResource("datasources.yml")
                .addAsResource("META-INF/persistence.xml")
                .addAsResource("META-INF/load.sql")
                .addAsManifestResource(EmptyAsset.INSTANCE, "beans.xml");
    }

    @CreateSwarm
    public static Swarm createSwarm() throws Exception {
        Swarm swarm = new Swarm();
        ClassLoader cl = CatalogServiceTest.class.getClassLoader();
        URL dataSourcesConfig = cl.getResource("datasources.yml");
        swarm.withConfig(dataSourcesConfig);
        return swarm;
    }

    //2
    private static Client client;

    //3
    @BeforeClass
    public static void setUpClient() {
        client = ClientBuilder.newClient();
    }

    //4
    @ArquillianResource
    private URL url;

    //5
    private Item testEndpoint(String itemId) {
        WebTarget target = client.target(url + "item/"+itemId);
        return target.request("application/json").get(Item.class);
    }

    @Test
    //6
    @RunAsClient
    public void testSearchById() {
        //7
        Assert.assertEquals(testEndpoint("turtle").getName(),"turtle");
        Assert.assertEquals(testEndpoint("hamster").getName(),"hamster");
    }
}
```

There is quite a bit of stuff that we had to implement. Let's analyze it one by one.

As we are going to test the REST endpoint, we have to add classes that will expose it, that is, `CatalogResource` and `CatalogApplication` (1).

Arquillian is able to find out the URL of a created service and inject it into the test. To obtain such an object, we have to annotate the URL field with the `org.jboss.arquillian.test.api.ArquillianResource` annotation (4).

We have implemented the convenience test method, which makes invocations to the service and obtains item instances, based on the ID (5).

The most important addition to the test is annotating the `test` methods with the `org.jboss.arquillian.container.test.api.RunAsClient` annotation. As a result, the test will run from Maven's JVM as a standalone client. We are using the test annotated in this way in order to create a test that will assert the correct behavior of our service, based on invocations from the test JVM (6).

Summary

In this chapter, you learned what Arquillian is and how you can use it to test Swarm microservices. You also learned how to configure Arquillian to automatically create a Swarm container, how to modify the container configuration, and how to test the created microservice from within the container and from a standalone client.

Further reading

`http://arquillian.org/`

6
Deploying Applications on the Cloud with OpenShift

In the previous chapters, we showed you how to develop microservices with WildFly Swarm. In this chapter, you will learn how to deploy those services to the cloud, and you will use OpenShift to achieve that. However, why should we bother? What are the features and benefits of cloud computing? Let's start by saying a few words about it.

Before we move on to the next section, you need to be provided with some important information. This chapter describes a lot of theoretical concepts that explain the internals of OpenShift. Don't worry if some of those concepts sound too complex to configure because (spoiler alert!), in the end, OpenShift will do most of the stuff for you. The goal of this chapter is to provide you with knowledge, which will allow you to understand all the magic that OpenShift can do, and. In later chapters, modify, and reconfigure that behavior. So, let's begin.

Cloud computing

OK. Let's start at the beginning. So, what actually is cloud computing?

Cloud computing is an IT paradigm that advocates the use of shared pools of configurable resources and services provided over the internet. Those services are provided on demand, rapidly, and with minimal management. As a result, cloud computing allows for flexible architecture, optimized resource usage, and the possibility of decoupling the infrastructure provider from a consumer, enabling the separation of concerns. Let's examine those statements in greater detail.

Resources provisioned on demand give you, as a developer or an architect, flexibility in configuring your technical infrastructure. Starting the project is cheap, as you don't have to begin with infrastructure investments. Also, when your project is in production, computing resources may be scaled automatically to fill your application's demands. In each case, you are paying only for the resources used.

Furthermore, cloud computing introduces the separation of concerns. The cloud provider becomes specialized in provisioning the infrastructure. The developers are provided with the interface of the cloud infrastructure and will use it for the development. As a result, they don't need to be concerned with the details of the infrastructure configuration as long as they comply with the interface provided by the cloud. Cloud providers, on the other hand, have to compete to provide the most convenient and robust cloud infrastructure while minimizing the costs.

Throughout this chapter, we will describe the cloud interface provided by OpenShift. Before that, we will describe the following two cloud infrastructure characteristics, which will enable the use of a consistent set of concepts during the following chapters: deployment and service models. Let's start with the first one.

The cloud infrastructure deployment model

The cloud deployment model specifies how cloud infrastructure is organized. Let's look at commonly used models.

The public cloud

The **public cloud** is a model in which services are provided over a network for public usage.

Public cloud computing is sometimes described as an evolution of computing resources into utility such as electricity. Using the example of a power provider may give you an alternative insight into the topics described in this paragraph: the power distribution company is responsible, among other, for ensuring that the network can deal with demand peaks, or provide network redundancy in case of traction breakdown. However, in the end, we don't think about it too much—we insert the plug into the socket when needed and get billed only for electricity we used.

We shouldn't stretch that analogy too far though. Computing resources are obviously not a commodity like electricity, and they cannot be provided to everyone in a uniform manner because of different customer requirements.

First of all, not all customers are able, for various reasons, to move their workloads to the public cloud. One of the reasons may be the need for a higher level of security or greater control over the architecture. Such customers can take advantage of the private cloud discuss it.

The private cloud

In the **private cloud**, the computing resources used to create the cloud are dedicated to a single customer. The resources may be located on-site or off-site, owned by the customer, or managed by a third party. All of the resources are provisioned for a single client and are not shared by multiple clients. Such a configuration allows for greater control and security but requires the company to invest in and manage the cloud resources, removing the decoupling benefit of the public cloud.

The hybrid cloud

The **hybrid cloud** is a model in which public and private clouds are connected together. As a result, you can take advantage of both solutions. For example, you can run services that deal with sensitive data on the private cloud, but use the public cloud to scale other services.

 We would like our cloud provider to provide cloud abstraction that will enable users to see a homogeneous cloud view, abstracting away the infrastructure details of the hybrid cloud. We will return to this thought later, when we describe the architecture of OpenShift.

Let's now focus on another cloud characteristic, that is, the **service model**.

The service model

As you learned at the beginning of this chapter, the cloud provider is responsible for providing computing resources on demand. Computing resources can be provisioned in different ways, and characterized by different levels of abstraction. This feature of cloud computing infrastructure is called a service model. Let's describe the commonly used models.

Infrastructure as a Service

In **Infrastructure as a Service (IaaS)**, a customer is able to install arbitrary applications (including operating systems) on the provisioned resources. The customer does not control the infrastructure that is provided by the cloud provider. For example, the customer may get access to a remote virtual machine, which they can fully operate.

Platform as a Service

In **Platform as a Service (PaaS)**, as its name suggests, the cloud provider is responsible for providing the customer with a ready-for-use the platform on which the customer can deploy and run their applications. Let's suppose that you want to use the database. In this case, the platform provider is responsible for giving you access to an up-to-date and configured database on which you can start working immediately. You don't have to mess with the entire configuration, and can start working with the database (or any other technology; WildFly Swarm, for example) straightaway.

Software as a Service

Finally, there is **Software as a Service (SaaS)**. In this model, the customer is able to use the application provided by the cloud provider. An example of SaaS may be disc storage, email, or an office suite provided over the internet.

OK, now that we've clarified the nomenclature, we can finally dig into OpenShift architecture.

The OpenShift architecture

So far, we have been talking in abstract terms. In this section, we will give you an overview of the OpenShift architecture. As a result, you will gain a practical understanding of the functioning cloud PaaS infrastructure.

Let's start with a bird's-eye view architecture diagram:

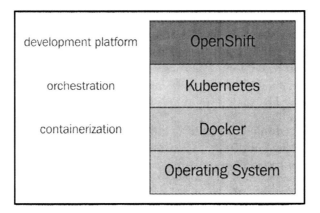

The preceding diagram sketches the layers of OpenShift architecture. **Docker** runs on top of the operating system and provides layers of containers. Containers are lightweight, standalone, and executable pieces of software (*Further reading*, link 2) that can be run anywhere on the cloud. Those containers are orchestrated by **Kubernetes**, which provides a unified view of heterogeneous computing resources. Finally, **OpenShift** builds on top of **Kubernetes**, providing developer tools that automate most configuration tasks. If this short description sounded cryptic to you, don't worry. Everything will be clear by the end of this chapter. Let's start with containers.

Containerization

As we said before, in cloud computing, the cloud provider is responsible for providing the server resources to users on demand. However, what does that actually mean? How are those resources provided? How is the server with all the necessary configurations created, and how it is isolated from other users? To understand this, we must understand how containers work.

Containers are basically a type of **virtualization**. Let's discuss this concept.

Virtualization

Virtualization is a technology that allows the running of many isolated virtual machines on one server. A virtual machine is an emulation of a computer system governed by the virtualization application running on the server's operating system. The user to whom the virtual machine has been provisioned has access to the fully operational host. The fact that the host is not physical, and that it shares the resources of the physical server with other virtual machines, is being abstracted away from the user.

Another key feature of virtualization is the ability to serialize the virtual machine into the image. This feature enables portability. The image can be moved to different servers, thus ensuring that the state of the virtual machine will be preserved.

Why is virtualization important to the cloud provider, then?

Firstly, the cloud provider is able to provide access to the virtual machine to the user. As a result, the user will obtain access to a fraction of server resources. From the user's perspective, they will have access to the isolated server

Secondly, the user has the ability to use a preconfigured image of the platform that they want to use. Do you need Fedora with WildFly AS? Here is your configured image. We will run it on our server, and you are ready to go.

Thirdly, the cloud provider is able to optimize the resource usage. There can be many virtual machines running on one server, minimizing the idle time.

Fourthly, Virtual machines can be moved freely between different servers when necessary. If more resources are needed, some virtual machines can be transferred to another server. Again, from the user's point of view, you will have access to an isolated preconfigured server and won't have to worry about the details.

Then, what about the implementation?

Some of you may identify virtualization with hardware (of full) virtualization. In this architecture, the virtualization application is responsible for emulating the whole operating system with all the necessary processes and libraries.

This solution has some performance problems, most of them resulting from the fact that the operating system was initially designed to run on a physical host. Firstly, to start the virtual machine the whole OS has to be started and, as a result, the startup time may be substantial (minutes). Secondly, OS processes and libraries have to be duplicated in each virtual machine, which leads to non-optimal resources usage.

Let's think about it from the cloud provider's perspective, taking special consideration of the microservices architecture that we described in `Chapter 1`, *Java EE and Modern Architectural Methodologies*. We would like to have a solution that will enable us to provide a large number of ephemeral virtual machines. We would like to ensure that they can be started and stopped immediately, optimizing the use of resources, and store image data effectively. It turns out that we need another tool. Let's discuss containers.

Containers

Containers are the implementation of a system-level virtualization (or paravirtualization). In this kind of virtualization, the operating system is not emulated on each virtual machine. Instead, virtual machines share the same operating system instance, using the tools provided by it to achieve isolation. As a result, in this model, we can think of virtual machines as isolated user-space instances running on top of the same operating system. Such instances are called container.

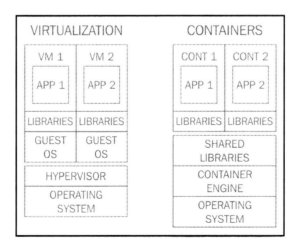

The preceding diagram highlights the main differences between full virtualization and containers. Containers share the same operating system and, as you will learn in the next sections, are able to share common libraries effectively. In the preceding diagram, the horizontal line represents the layers that have to be created when the new virtual machine/container is created.

Before we describe the Docker implementation of containers, let's talk about the isolation tools that the Linux kernel provides.

Kernel isolation tools

The Linux kernel provides a wide array of tools that enable the isolation of processes, and put a resource usage limit on those groups. The main tools that enable that (and are used by Docker containers) are namespaces (isolation), and `cgroups` (limits). Let's learn more about it.

Namespaces

Each kernel process can be assigned to a namespace—processes with the same namespace share the same view some of the system resources. For example, a PID namespace provides the ability to isolate processes—processes in the same PID namespace can see each other, but cannot see processes from different namespaces.

There is a group of namespaces in Linux kernel that provides PID, network, mount point, and username isolation.

cgroups

The `cgroups` are responsible for limiting the resource usage for the group of processes. `cgroups` allow you to assign processes to a number of groups and configure a resource quota for those groups. The resources that can be controlled are, among others, CPU, memory usage, network, and disk bandwidths. In the event of resource congestion, the `cgroups` mechanism will make sure that the group won't exceed its quota for that resource.

In the case of containers, a group may be created for each container. As a result, we would be able to provide a quota for all of the containers. We may, for example, assign 1/5 of the CPU to one of the containers. This would guarantee that, in the case of a congestion, this container would have access to that amount of the CPU cycles. As a result, we are able to guarantee resource access. The `cgroups` limit is only enforced during the congestion. In our example, if all other containers are idle, the container that was assigned a fraction of CPU quota may use more CPU cycles.

The Docker implementation of containers

You have just learned that the Linux kernel provides tools that enable isolation of resources, laying the ground for the following the implementation of system-level virtualization. But we have to ask ourselves some questions: which applications will be run inside the container? Which libraries and files will be visible in individual containers?

To answer these questions, we will introduce you to Docker images. As we have hinted at before, virtual machines in hardware virtualization can be stored as images, which make it possible to store the state of the virtual machine and, as a result, allow for the creation of reusable preconfigured virtual machines and portability.

The same feature concerns containers and the implementation that we will use: Docker. As you will learn in the following sections, this idea has been developed to a whole different level, providing us with an efficient and convenient image ecosystem and, as a result it, provides a base environment for our cloud infrastructure. However, let's start at the beginning.

Images and containers

In Docker nomenclature, there is a distinction between an image and a container. An image is an immutable, unambiguously identifiable collection of files and metadata. A container, on the other hand, is a runtime instance of an image. There can be many container instances of the same image, each of which is mutable and has its own state.

Let's make it clear it with the help of an example. You can start a Fedora distribution in a container. To do so, you have to download and build a Fedora image. After the build, the image will be located on your machine and will contain the Fedora distribution. As we mentioned in the preceding paragraph, this image is an immutable template that can be used to start a container. When you start the container based on the Fedora image and log in to it, you will see that you have access to the bare Fedora distribution. You can, among other things, install software and create files there. When you do this, you modify only that specific container. If you run another container from the same Fedora image, you will again have access to the bare Fedora distribution.

The preceding example gives you a bird's-eye view of the behavior of containers and images. Let's now take a closer look at the architecture of both.

Images are described by `Dockerfiles`. A `Dockerfile` is a text file, which contains a list of commands that instruct you on how to assemble an image.

Images have a layered structure. The commands executed in a `Dockerfile` result in the creation of additional layers—every subsequent layer is different from the previous one.

Every image must derive from another image (possibly, an explicitly empty *scratch* image), and it adds its layers on top of it. Image layers are built directly on top of the kernel code.

Let's clarify all those concepts by taking a look at a practical example. We will create a bunch of simple images.

Firstly, we will create a number of files in the local directory from which we will build the images:

```
.
├── base
│   └── Dockerfile
├── image1
│   ├── A
│   │   └── A.txt
│   ├── B
│   │   └── B.txt
│   └── Dockerfile
└── image2
    ├── C
    │   └── C.txt
    └── Dockerfile
```

Let's create the first image now (note that we are aiming at architecture description; so, although we will briefly explain the commands used, refer to (Further reading, link 1) if you are interested in the details):

```
FROM centos:7
RUN useradd -ms /bin/bash tomek
USER tomek
WORKDIR /home/tomek
```

The preceding `Dockerfile` represents the base image. It derives from the `centos:7` image, which is a bare Centos distribution, adds the `tomek` user (#2), and switches the previous user to `tomek` so that all subsequent commands will be run as this user (#3), therefore the directory from any further commands will be executed to `tomek`'s `homedir`.

In order to build an image from `Dockerfile`, we have to execute the following command in the directory in which the image is located:

docker build -t base

In the preceding command, we have tagged the image as base. As a result, we are able to refer to it by its base name. Let's move on to the second Dockerfile:

```
#1
FROM base
#2
COPY A A
#3
COPY B B
```

The preceding image derives from the base image created before that. It copies directories A (#2) and B (#3) from our local filesystem to the image. Similarly, let's build and tag the image:

```
docker build -t middle .
```

Finally, take a look at the last image:

```
#1
FROM middle
#2
COPY C C
```

It derives from the middle image (#1) and copies the C directory (#2) from the local filesystem to the image.

The following diagram presents the layers of the top image. We have included all the commands from the image hierarchy so that you can take a look at how the top image is assembled from scratch:

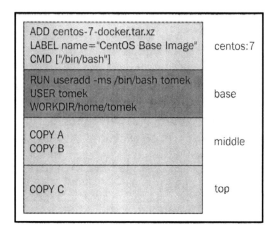

As you will notice in the preceding diagram, each command from all the `Dockerfiles` is translated into an additional layer. The base image, for example, derives from the `centos:7` images and, as a result, its first layer is added on top of `centos` layers. Similarly, the top image is based on the middle image, and as a result, the layer resulting from the execution of the `COPY C` command is added on top of layers from the middle image.

We now understand how `Dockerfiles` translate to the image layer structure. However, why is this structure important? It is important because it enables images to share the layers. Let's find out how.

When we build the image, the commands from the `Dockerfile` will be executed and all the layers will be created. As you saw in the preceding example, images are connected to each other and can share layers. A layer that is used by multiple images has to be created only once.

In the preceding example, the middle and top images share all the layers from the middle image. If we decide to build the middle image, all its layers will also be created. If we later build the top image, none of the middle layers have to be created again.

To understand why such sharing of layers is possible, we must understand how the layers influence filesystem behavior after the container is started.

When we start the container based on an image, we are inserting another layer on top of an image from which the container was started. The container will write its changes to this layer, but the result won't change the image, which is immutable. To understand why this is the case, we must understand how layers influence filesystem behavior at runtime. Let's find out.

When Docker starts a container, it creates a filesystem that will be mounted as the root filesystem of the container. Such a filesystem overlays all the layers from the image and the writable layer, creating the filesystem that appears to combine the files and directories from all the layers that constitute the image. Let's return to our example to show how it works.

Let's create three containers based on the images from our previous example:

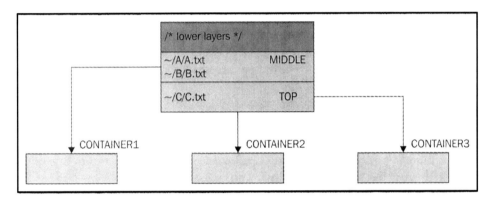

In the preceding diagram, the top rectangle represents the images that we have created. The middle image has added two layers corresponding to directories A and B. The top image has added one layer with the C directory. There are three containers. Two containers (**2** and **3**) are based on the top image, and **CONTAINER1** is based on the middle image. The rectangles at the bottom represent each container's writable layer.

Since all layers have been combined into one filesystem, all containers will see the whole operating system distribution. The content of the home directory will be different for **CONTAINER1**, **CONTAINER2**, and **CONTAINER3**: **CONTAINER1** will see only A and B directories in its home folder, whereas **CONTAINER2** and **CONTAINER3** will see A, B, and C directories.

Let's explain how this overlay is implemented. When a container reads a file, the storage driver (a component responsible for the union filesystem implementation) looks for that file starting from the top layer. If the file is not found, it moves to the layer below it. The cycle repeats till either the file is found or there are no more layers. If a file is not found in any of the layers, we will get a `File not found` error.

Let's suppose that **CONTAINER1** wants to read a `~/C/c.txt` file. The storage driver starts searching in **CONTAINER3**'s writable layer. Since the file is not there, it moves to the `COPY C` layer from the top image. The file is found there and is read.

What happens if **CONTAINER1** wants to read the same file?

The storage driver starts from **CONTAINER1**'s writable layer. Again, it cannot find the file, but this time it moves to the `COPY B` layer, which is the top layer of the middle image from which the container was created. The file cannot be found there, nor in any layers below it. We will end up with a `File not found` a message.

What if **CONTAINER1** and **CONTAINER2** want to read `~/B/b.txt`?

After reading the supposition in the preceding paragraph, you will know that both files can be read. Note, however, that both containers were reading the same file. The `"COPY B"` layer is reused by the middle and top images, and the `b.txt` file reads from the same image for both containers. Thanks to layers, containers are able to reuse data.

Now, what about writing to a file?

The storage controller uses a copy-on-write strategy when writing a file to a filesystem. The driver looks for a file in all the layers, again from top to bottom. If the file is present in the container's writable layer, it can be directly open for write. If it is present in one of the image's layers, it is copied to a writable layer and opened for write.

Let's return to our example. Let's suppose that **CONTAINER1** wants to write to the `~/A/a.txt` file:

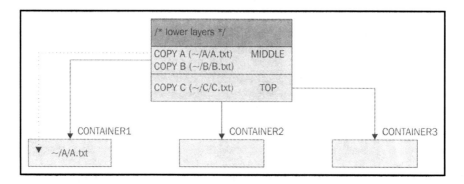

The storage driver has found the `~/A/A.txt` file in **COPY A** layer and copied it to the writable layer of **CONTAINER1**. Subsequent reads and writes of the `~/A/A.txt` file from **CONTAINER1** will read/write the file from **CONTAINER1**'s writable layer.

Let's suppose that **CONTAINER3** wants to write to the ~/A/A.txt file:

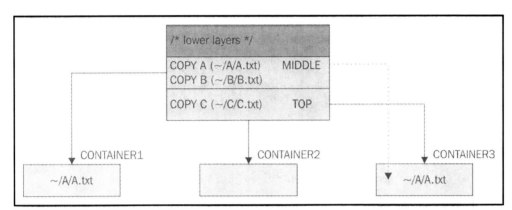

The situation is analogous; the file is copied to **CONTAINER3**'s writable layer. Let's look at the current situation. Each container has had access to the Fedora distribution and modified some of its parts.

CONTAINER1 and **CONTAINER3** still share most of the data, as only the files modified by the given container are copied to its writable layer.

As you will noticed in the preceding diagram, the implementation of Docker images provides an effective way of storing multiple images on the same host. Then, what about container startup time? The container uses the resources of the underlying Linux kernel and reuses the image layers (provided that they are present—if not, they are downloaded only once). Because of that, starting the container means creating a writable layer and running the container processes using Kernel isolation features. As you are able to see, such processes are very lightweight compared to the hardware virtualization. As a result, containers can be started and stopped immediately.

By this point, we have described the implications of Docker image architecture on container virtualization performance. You may have doubts regarding the performance of such an implementation in other circumstances. Surely, a layered filesystem would have a performance penalty if we decided to run a database on it. That's a good point that has to be clarified. A Docker-layered filesystem is used to work effectively with Docker containers. The layered filesystem is not meant to store data that requires high performance; this is the role of volumes, which we will learn about in the next chapter.

There may be different implementations of a storage driver. For example, copy on write strategy may be implemented on the file or page-cache level. Docker provides a number of implementations, and choosing the correct one depends on your use case.

If you are interested in the architecture of specific storage drivers, or you are researching which driver is best for your use case, refer to the Docker documentation.

Docker registries

Let's return to the build process of our example container. When we were building the base image for the first time, the following could be seen in the build log:

```
Step 1 : FROM fedora:26
Trying to pull repository docker.io/library/fedora ...
sha256:b27b4c551b1d06be25a3c76c1a9ceefd7ff189f6f8b1711d3e4b230c2081bff3:
Pulling from docker.io/library/fedora
Digest:
sha256:b27b4c551b1d06be25a3c76c1a9ceefd7ff189f6f8b1711d3e4b230c2081bff3
Status: Downloaded newer image for docker.io/fedora:26
(...)
```

As it turns out, the `fedora:26` images were downloaded from the `docker.io` server. Which service that enables users to download images?

Docker images, just like Maven artifacts or operating system packages, create an ecosystem of interconnected reusable entities. Just like in a Maven or operating system scenario, we need a service that will store and distribute such images. Such service is called a Docker registry.

Docker provides a default registry called DockerHub. DockerHub is a publicly available free registry. If not configured, Docker will use DockerHub as the default registry.

Docker wrap-up

As you can see, Docker is a tool that provides a number of capabilities that are essential building blocks for our cloud architecture, as follows:

- The isolation implemented on the operating system level, combined with a layered filesystem implementation, makes it possible to share server resources effectively and allows for immediate container startup.

- The image ecosystem provides a vast number of images that can be downloaded and used immediately.
- The containers run from the same images and operate on different Docker environments, providing consistency in all your environments. As you will learn in the rest of this chapter, this is the key feature of a dynamic cloud environment.

All these features make Docker containers a great building block for cloud infrastructure. However, we need more than that. First, there will be a lot of containers in nontrivial environments. We are aiming for a dynamic environment, which enables, among other things, automatic scaling, high availability, and continuous integration as we expect a large number of those containers to be started and stopped within short periods of time. Finally, no matter how cool and efficient Docker images are, we would preferably like to generate them automatically during the build of our applications. All of those issues are resolved for you by OpenShift. Let's continue learning about the OpenShift stack. The next thing that you need to learn is orchestration.

Orchestrating Docker

We have just learned about a tool that enables us to provide the containers—lightweight, virtual machines using operating system-level virtualization and providing us with isolation, effective resource usage, immediate creation time, and the most repeatable behavior across different environments. This is the first layer in our cloud environment, but it is not our target platform. In a more complex production system, we would have to manage a large number of containers and, obviously, we don't want to do it manually. We will need a tool that will manage our containers in a clever way. Let's meet Kubernetes.

Kubernetes

In order to show you the interface that Kubernetes provides, let's introduce its main architectural concepts.

Nodes and master services

Kubernetes creates a cluster from a group of computers. The computers that constitute the cluster can be heterogeneous. A cluster may be created on your laptop, a group of workstations, or virtual machines. Also, all types of worker machines can be mixed in one cluster.

In Kubernetes nomenclature, each worker machine is a node and the whole cluster is governed by the master node. Each node runs the Kubelet, which is a daemon that enables communication with the master and the Docker engine so that Kubernetes can deploy containers on it.

The master, on the other hand, is a group of services that coordinate the whole cluster. From the user's point of view, the most important part of the master is its REST API service, which provides an endpoint that allows users to interact with the whole cluster.

The following diagram presents a sample Kubernetes cluster, which we will use in the further description. The master services are represented by the blue circle and each node is represented by a rectangle. The cluster consists of two workstations (cyan), two virtual machines (green), and one laptop. Each node runs Kubelet so that it can connect with the master, and the Docker engine so that it can start containers:

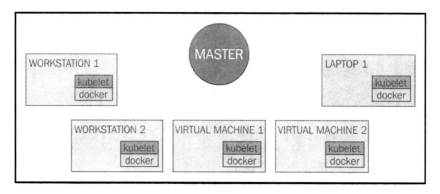

Volumes

In Kubernetes, containers are ephemeral which means that they may be started and stopped often. If the container data is not committed, it will be erased when the container is stopped. As a result, we will need another tool for the storage of data. In Kubernetes, such a functionality is provided by volumes. Volume is a persistent storage implementation, which has an independent life cycle and can be mounted in a number of containers. We will discuss volumes in detail in the next chapter.

Pods

In Kubernetes, a pod is a group of containers and volumes, all of which share the same IP address among the cluster.

All content of the pod is guaranteed to run on the same host. As a result, a pod can be thought of as an atomic unit of deployment and scheduling.

The pod concept is needed in order to provide us with the ability to implement decoupled containers. With pods, we are able to collocate a bunch of containers with different functionalities that have to be located together (and possibly share data). Those distinct functionalities can be encapsulated in each container. If, on the other hand, a container would have to be used as an atomic unit of deployment, we may be forced to collocate distinct functionalities in one container in order to ensure that they will be deployed and scaled together, breaking good design principles of low coupling and high cohesion.

In a large number of scenarios, a pod will contain only one container, and this will be perfectly fine. Pods don't have to comprise many containers, but you are provided with such a possibility so that you can use it when it is necessary for your application.

Deployments

We already know about the building blocks of a Kubernetes cluster. Now it's time to look at the thing that interests us the most: deploying applications to it.

When you want to deploy an application to the Kubernetes cluster, you have to create the deployment object that contains information about it. Among other things, Kubernetes must know which containers constitute the pod and how many replicas of the pod have to be created. Given that knowledge, Kubernetes will decide on which node's application pods will be deployed, and it will deploy them there:

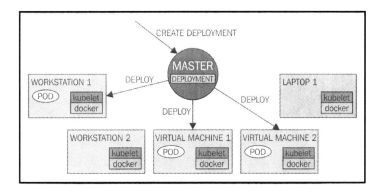

In the preceding diagram, the deployment, which requires that the pod be replicated on three hosts, has been created. Let's assume that Kubernetes has decided that the pod will be run on **WORKSTATION1** and the two virtual machines. The deployment object has become a part of the master model. What do we actually mean by that?

It has to be strongly emphasized that deployment isn't an operation that will finish after execution, leaving no further impact on the cluster status. Instead, the deployment effectively adds objects to the description of the desired state of the cluster. It is the role of Kubernetes to make sure that this state will be maintained.

We have hinted that Kubernetes master provides the REST API. This API allows for the creation of an object describing the desired state of the cluster. The deployment is one of those objects. As a result, deploying an application to the cluster is the equivalent of adding one more deployment object to the cluster description.

Kubernetes monitors the state of the cluster and is responsible for making sure that it is equivalent to that description. To clarify it a little more, let's look at a few simple examples.

Let's suppose that one node in the cluster has gone down. As a result, the group of pods that were deployed on it has to be moved to different nodes so that the number of deployed pods matches the description of the deployment. To present it in our example, let's suppose that **VIRTUAL MACHINE 1** has gone down:

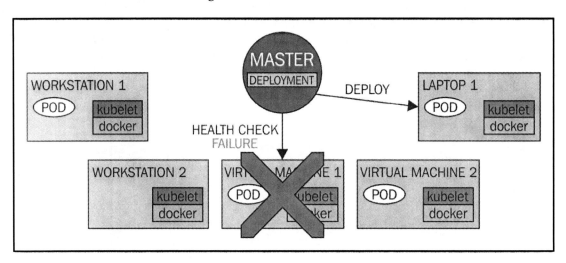

In such a scenario, master would find out that the **VIRTUAL MACHINE 1** node has failed and, in order to keep the number of pod replicas aligned with the description, it will deploy one more pod on another machine—**LAPTOP 1**, in our example.

Then, what about deploying a new version of an application? We would have to change the version in the deployment description. Kubernetes will find out that the version has changed. It will roll down the pods with the preceding version of an application and start pods with the new application. Let's present this example in our diagram:

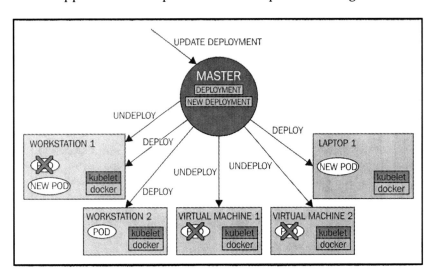

Kubernetes has undeployed the pods that constitute the preceding application, replaced the old deployment object with the new one, chosen on which nodes the updated pods have to be deployed, and, finally, performed deployment on those nodes.

 Because this chapter is aimed at explaining OpenShift architecture, we are using general theoretical examples. We will show you how scaling and deployments are done in practical examples in the following chapters.

The key point to understand now is the principle on which Kubernetes operates: it is responsible for keeping the cluster synchronized with the desired state described by the user.

Services

You may already have noticed that there is a problem with the dynamic pod deployments described in the preceding section. How are we supposed to connect to the application if we have no idea where its pods are located? To solve this problem, Kubernetes introduced the service concept.

A service is an object that monitors the group of pods that constitutes an application. It contains search criteria that define which pods are the part of an application, and monitors the cluster so that it knows where these pods are located. A service has its own IP address, which is visible from outside the cluster. As a result, the client only has to know the address of a service. The actual cluster status (number of pods and their location) is abstracted away from the client.

Let's present it again in our example:

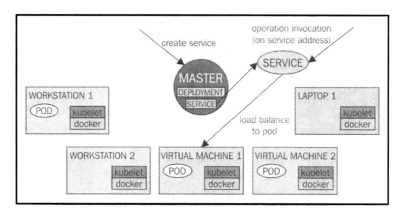

In the preceding diagram, the call to the master has created the service object in the master's object model, which has resulted in the creation of the service. The created service has an IP address, which is reachable by the external clients. When invoked, the service will load balance the invocation to one of the pods from the cluster. Note that the service constantly monitors the state of the cluster. If, for example, there is a failure in one of the nodes, the service will learn the new locations of the pods and will continue to work correctly.

This example combines together all the concepts that we have introduced. Let's recap them: Kubernetes creates a cluster of heterogeneous worker machines. All machines in a cluster have to be able to run Docker containers and communicate with Kubernetes master services that govern all the clusters. The unit of deployment is a pod, which consists of one or more containers and can have many replicas. A user creates the description of such deployments using the master's API, and Kubernetes is responsible for ensuring that the actual cluster state matches this description. To do that, it has to, among other things, perform health checks of nodes and the application, and redeploy them as necessary. It also has to react to all model changes and modify the cluster accordingly. Owing to all the reasons mentioned in this paragraph, application pods can be located on different nodes, and those locations can change dynamically. As a result, Kubernetes introduces the service concept, which provides the proxy for the external clients to the pods that constitute the application to which the client wants to connect.

Labels

Each object in a OpenShift cluster model can have any number of labels, which are basically key-value properties. This is a very simple, yet powerful, feature.

We will need a way to be able to categorize different types of objects. We can build a directory structure for that, but the problem with that solution is that it's not flexible enough. A directory structure provides one view of objects, but there may be many of them, depending on the user or on the current usage scenario.

Labels, on the other hand, provide full flexibility. Any object can have any number of labels applied. Those labels can be used in queries to find an OpenShift object based on a wide range of characteristics.

As an example, let's take a look at a service object again. The service has to find all the pods that run the application represented by the service. The service finds those pods by querying the labels: it's a common practice for the pod to have an app label set to the name of an application that runs on it. As a result, the service can query for pods with an appropriate app label.

Benefits

Now that we know the most important concepts regarding the architecture of Kubernetes, it is time to look at the big picture of the interface that it provides. Kubernetes takes the group of heterogeneous worker machines and provides its user with a view of a homogeneous container execution environment. Let's think about this for a moment. As a user, you tell Kubernetes, *I want to deploy my application, which consists of N pods.* Kubernes will place those somewhere in the cluster. If pods have to be scaled up or down, or if there are failures, Kubernetes will take care of moving those pods between the underlying machines, but the technical details of those machines are abstracted away from the user. With Kubernetes, a user sees the cluster as a pool of container execution resources. Furthermore, this view is the same for all the clusters that you may want to run in your environment. The Kubernetes development cluster on your laptop will have the same interface as your production environment.

We must also emphasize the role that containers play—Docker guarantees that two containers built from the same image will behave identically. Combining that fact with the role that Kubernetes plays, we are able to see the cloud view provided by Docker and Kubernetes: a pool of container execution computing resources, which further guarantees repeatable behavior on all environments on which it is deployed.

OpenShift

In the previous sections, we covered the powerful cloud abstraction that is provided by Kubernetes and Docker. On the other hand, we hinted in a number of places that in order to use Kubernetes effectively, you have to, among other things, deal directly with Kubernetes object configurations or Docker files. As we wrote before, we would preferably like to have a tool that will abstract those things away from us, make them either happen automatically, or be configured using easy-to-use tools. Here is where OpenShift steps in. OpenShift adds another layer of abstraction on top of Kubernetes, providing it with additional cluster model features, such as builds, or tools, such as web console. As you will see, the layer added by OpenShift makes all the cloud operations very simple and effectively allows you to focus on the development of your code.

Returning for a moment to the cloud computing types section at the beginning of this chapter, we can say that Kubernetes and Docker provide you with IaaS, whereas OpenShift transforms it into powerful programmer-oriented PaaS.

You will learn about the most important features provided by OpenShift in the following paragraphs. Now, let's quickly highlight the most important features of OpenShift. We will start with the build infrastructure.

The build infrastructure

In the previous paragraphs, we suggested that direct Docker images are abstracted away by OpenShift. Now it's time to look at it a little more closely.

OpenShift provides builds and deployment abstractions. Builds are responsible for creating images, and deployments are responsible for deploying those images to the cluster, providing the abstraction above Kubernetes objects, such as replication controllers.

One of the first questions that come to mind now is how are those images built? There are a bunch of options, but the most interesting one for us is source-to-image build. As its name suggests, this kind of build is responsible for automatically turning your code into a Docker image.

As a result, your interaction with OpenShift may be configured as follows: you write your application and push the changes into the GitHub repository. This triggers the source-to-image build, which creates a Docker image, and the creation of the Docker image may trigger automatic deployment. Also, all those steps may be integrated into Jenkins based on a continuous delivery pipeline. As you can see, OpenShift build tools allow you to concentrate only on code development. The interaction with cloud will be done automatically by the build infrastructure.

You will learn more about deployments and about builds (including source-to-image and pipeline builds) in `Chapter 9`, *Configuring Continuous Integration Using Jenkins*.

Management of projects and users

This feature is not as fresh as the preceding one, but it's still very important. In order to make OpenShift able to work in an enterprise environment, the concept of the project is necessary.

Kubernetes provides the namespace concept, which enables it to separate the cluster into a group of virtual clusters. This concept namespace doesn't implement access control though. As a result, OpenShift creates the notion of a project, which is a Kubernetes namespace identified by specific annotation and implementing access control policies based on users and user groups.

You will learn more about security microservice applications in `Chapter 10`, *Providing Security Using Keycloak*.

Minishift

We have already said a lot of good things about OpenShift. It is high time we saw how it works in practice. However, how are you actually able to do that? As a developer, you have access to OpenShift Online. It is a publicly available OpenShift cloud where anyone can open an account and test OpenShift itself.

There is also another option: Minishift. Minishiftis a tool that starts a virtual machine on your local computer and creates an OpenShift cluster inside it. As a result, it enables you to try and test a fully featured OpenShift cluster on your local machine. This is the option that we will use in this book. Let's start by installing it.

Installation

You are able to download its latest version from the GitHub page. You also have to install the virtual machine that you will use and configure your environment variables accordingly. The process is very simple and takes a few minutes to complete. The details of the particular installation steps differ a bit between operating systems. They are described thoroughly in the attached installation guide.

Starting the cluster

After you have installed the cluster, you can start it using the minishift start command. It is a good practice to boost the default parameters to provide enough memory and disk space for the services that we will develop and use:

```
minishift start --memory=4096 --disk-size=30gb
```

After you run the preceding command, you have to wait few minutes for the cluster to start:

```
[root@fedoralaptop tomek]# su tomek
[tomek@fedoralaptop ~]$ minishift start
-- Checking if KVM driver is installed ...
   Driver is available at /usr/local/bin/docker-machine-driver-kvm ...
   Checking driver binary is executable ... OK
-- Starting local OpenShift cluster using 'kvm' hypervisor ...
-- Starting Minishift VM .............. OK
-- Checking for IP address ... OK
-- Checking if external host is reachable from the Minishift VM ...
   Pinging 8.8.8.8 ... OK
-- Checking HTTP connectivity from the VM ...
   Retrieving http://minishift.io/index.html ... OK
-- Checking if persistent storage volume is mounted ... OK
-- Checking available disk space ... 53% OK
-- OpenShift cluster will be configured with ...
   Version: v3.6.0
-- Checking `oc` support for startup flags ...
   host-data-dir ... OK
   host-pv-dir ... OK
   host-volumes-dir ... OK
   routing-suffix ... OK
   host-config-dir ... OK
Starting OpenShift using openshift/origin:v3.6.0 ...
OpenShift server started.

The server is accessible via web console at:
    https://192.168.42.201:8443
```

After minishift has started, we can access it using the provided address in the startup log. The first screen is a login screen. On this screen, you can use any credentials (as Minishift is a test tool) and click the **Login** button. After you do this, you will see the web console, which is one way of managing the OpenShift cluster. Let's learn more about it.

Web console

A web console is a graphical tool that enables you to view and manage the content of an OpenShift project. From a technical point of view, the console is a graphical interface that provides convenient abstraction over the OpenShift REST API, which it uses to modify the cluster model according to user operations.

Let's take a look at the main console window:

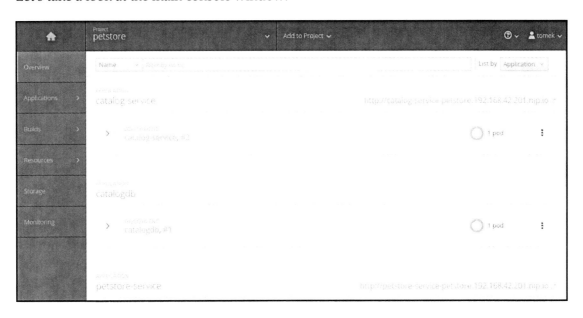

As you can see in the preceding screenshot, the console allows you to manage projects, view their content, and modify it. The overview (presented in the preceding screenshot) contains an application deployed in the petstore namespace. The menu on the left allows you to view and modify different aspects of the cluster, such as builds, deployments, or persistent resources.

We will use the web console extensively in the following chapters, where you will be able to take a look at most of its features and capabilities.

YAML notation

Although the majority of configuration can be done using the graphical interface, sometimes it will be necessary to edit the internal representation of OpenShift objects: YAML.

Each object in an OpenShift model can be represented using this kind of notation. If you click on **Applications** | **Deployments**, choose one of them, click on **Actions** in the top-right corner, you will be able to choose the **Edit YAML** option. This applies to all objects in the console.

We will be performing this from time to time when such an edit is necessary, informing you about the meaning of the performed operation.

CLI

Sometimes, it is more convenient to use a command-line tool instead of graphical interface. OpenShift provides it too. The OpenShift CLI implements the oc command-line tool, which allows for managing the cluster from the terminal.

You can install the CLI using the instruction provided in.

The first thing that you have to do in order to use oc is to log in to the cluster, as follows:

```
oc login
```

You will be asked for your credentials, and will have to provide the same credentials that were used to create your project in the web console.

There are a number of operations that the oc tool provides. We will use it extensively to get and describe operations. Let's introduce them now.

The get operation allows you to obtain available information about the availability of a given type of object; let's invoke the command:

```
oc get
```

The tool will suggest a type of object that you can inspect; let's take a look:

```
You must specify the type of resource to get. Valid resource types include:

    * all
    * buildconfigs (aka 'bc')
    * builds
    * certificatesigningrequests (aka 'csr')
    * clusters (valid only for federation apiservers)
    * clusterrolebindings
    * clusterroles
    * componentstatuses (aka 'cs')
    * configmaps (aka 'cm')
    * daemonsets (aka 'ds')
    * deployments (aka 'deploy')
    * deploymentconfigs (aka 'dc')
    * endpoints (aka 'ep')
    * events (aka 'ev')
    * horizontalpodautoscalers (aka 'hpa')
    * imagestreamimages (aka 'isimage')
    * imagestreams (aka 'is')
    * imagestreamtags (aka 'istag')
    * ingresses (aka 'ing')
    * groups
    * jobs
    * limitranges (aka 'limits')
    * namespaces (aka 'ns')
    * networkpolicies
    * nodes (aka 'no')
    * persistentvolumeclaims (aka 'pvc')
    * persistentvolumes (aka 'pv')
    * poddisruptionbudgets (aka 'pdb')
    * podpreset
    * pods (aka 'po')
    * podsecuritypolicies (aka 'psp')
    * podtemplates
    * policies
    * projects
    * replicasets (aka 'rs')
    * replicationcontrollers (aka 'rc')
    * resourcequotas (aka 'quota')
    * rolebindings
    * roles
    * routes
    * secrets
    * serviceaccounts (aka 'sa')
    * services (aka 'svc')
    * statefulsets
    * users
    * storageclasses
    * thirdpartyresources
```

Wow! That's a lot, but don't worry, you will learn a lot about most of these in the next chapters. Let's use the `oc get` command to inspect the services available in the cluster:

```
[tomek@fedoralaptop ~]$ oc get svc
NAME              CLUSTER-IP       EXTERNAL-IP      PORT(S)              AGE
catalog-service   172.30.57.46     <none>           8080/TCP,8888/TCP    10d
catalogdb         172.30.121.1     <none>           5432/TCP             10d
payment-service                    192.168.1.144                         9d
petstore-service  172.30.104.170   <none>           8080/TCP,8888/TCP    10d
pricing-service   172.30.11.68     <none>           8080/TCP,8888/TCP    8d
pricingdb         172.30.138.42    <none>           5432/TCP             10d
[tomek@fedoralaptop ~]$ oc get svc/catalog-service
NAME              CLUSTER-IP       EXTERNAL-IP      PORT(S)              AGE
catalog-service   172.30.57.46     <none>           8080/TCP,8888/TCP    10d
[tomek@fedoralaptop ~]$ 
```

You can also take advantage of labels. If you write:

```
oc get all -l app=catalog-service
```

Then you will be able to see all kinds of objects associated with the service.

As you can see in the preceding code, we are able to list the objects that we are interested in using the `get` command. If we want to get some more information about them, we need to use the `oc describe` command, as follows:

```
[tomek@fedoralaptop ~]$ oc describe svc/catalog-service
Name:              catalog-service
Namespace:         petstore
Labels:            app=catalog-service
Annotations:       openshift.io/generated-by=OpenShiftNewApp
Selector:          app=catalog-service,deploymentconfig=catalog-service
Type:              ClusterIP
IP:                172.30.57.46
Port:              8080-tcp        8080/TCP
Endpoints:         172.17.0.5:8080
Port:              8888-tcp        8888/TCP
Endpoints:         172.17.0.5:8888
Session Affinity:  None
Events:            <none>
[tomek@fedoralaptop ~]$ 
```

The describe command allows you to read all the information about the given type of object.

You have now learned all the essential information needed to understand OpenShift. Now, it's finally time to try it.

Catalog-service on the OpenShift example

We have covered a lot of theory in this chapter and have introduced many concepts that will help you to better understand how OpenShift works under the hood. It is finally time to try it in practice.

We will deploy a `catalog-service` with a `h2` database. In this example, we will only use the web console and deploy the applications from the book's code repository.

Examples reference: `chapter6/catalog-service-openshift-h2`

Let's start. Let's enter the host address. You will find it in the log of the minishift start command. After entering it into the web browser, you will be welcomed by the user login screen. Let's enter our **Username** and **Password**.

We will be directed to the welcome screen, as follows:

Enter petstore as the name of the project. In order to deploy catalog-service to OpenShift, we will use the source-to-image build using the CLI. To start with, ensure that you have logged in to the cluster, as follows:

```
oc login
```

Then, you need to execute the following command:

```
oc create -f
https://raw.githubusercontent.com/wildfly-swarm/sti-wildflyswarm/master/1.0
/wildflyswarm-sti-all.json
```

The preceding command creates a bunch of OpenShift objects that are necessary to start an OpenShift build.

Finally, it is time to start an application:

```
oc new-app wildflyswarm-10-
centos7~https://github.com/PacktPublishing/Hands-On-Cloud-Development-with-
WildFly.git --context-dir=chapter6/catalog-service-openshift-h2/ --
name=catalog-service
```

We are fully aware that, at this point, these commands look cryptic. For some time, we will use them as a magical service deployment spell. Don't worry though, in Chapter 8, *Scaling and Connecting Your Services*, they will be fully explained, and you will be able to understand each part of the process. To give you a quick overview now: we are making OpenShift create a build of our service directly from source code. In order to do that, we have to specify the GitHub repository. Because our book repository contains many subdirectories, we have to specify the subdirectory in which this example is located—we use --context-dir for that. We also provide the name, using the --name command.

For now, let's use the web console to check whether the application has been deployed.

Login to the web console again and navigate to **Builds | Builds** on the left-hand side. You will be able to see that the build has indeed started:

Wait till the build has finished, then navigate to **Applications** | **Services**, and select **catalog-service**:

As you can see in the preceding screenshot, OpenShift has deployed the application on one pod and made a service for it.

Before we can check the application, we have to do one more simple thing. The services are not visible outside of the cluster, and as a result, in order to use them, we have to expose them on the address visible from the external network. OpenShift provides a tool that enables us to use these routes. In the preceding view, click on the **Create route** link, don't change anything, and click the **Create** button. After that, you will be able to see the external address of the service:

Route	Service Port	Target Port	Hostname
catalog-service	8080/TCP (8080-tcp)	8080	http://catalog-service-petstore.192.168.42.201.nip.io

Finally, we are ready to check the operation of our service. Copy the external address of the host and add the REST path to it:

It works. Congratulations! You have deployed your first service in OpenShift.

Summary

In this chapter, you learned a lot about OpenShift architecture. You were introduced to cloud computing and was provided the most essential information about it. Later, you learned about the architecture of OpenShift: a Kubernetes cluster using Docker images with an OpenShift layer, making cluster easy, to use and allowing developers to focus on coding.

Later in the chapter, you started your own local OpenShift instance using the Minishift tool and deployed your first service on it.

In the next chapter, you will learn how to configure persistent storage for microservices deployed in the cloud.

Further reading

1. https://docs.docker.com/engine/reference/builder/
2. https://www.docker.com/
3. https://openshift.io/
4. https://github.com/minishift/minishift
5. https://docs.openshift.org/latest/minishift/getting-started/installing.html
6. https://docs.openshift.com/enterprise/3.1/cli_reference/get_started_cli.html

7
Configuring Storage for Your Applications

In this chapter, we will start by learning the theoretical basis of OpenShift storage configuration. Later, we will show you how to deploy a database in the cloud and configure your cloud applications to use it.

In the last section of the preceding chapter, we deployed the simple version of CatalogService in the cloud, using OpenShift. We also got an initial feeling for the web console and OpenShift cli. Now, it is time to go further. We will reconfigure our application to use the database.

Before doing that, we will cover OpenShift persistence storage concepts.

OpenShift storage concepts

In the previous chapter, we hinted a the volume concept—the tool that is used by OpenShift to implement storage. Let's start by looking at it more thoroughly.

Volumes

As we mentioned in the preceding chapter, OpenShift's unit of deployment and scaling is a pod, which can contain many containers. The containers in the pod are ephemeral—they can be stopped and started at any moment by Kubernetes. The data stored in the container will be lost when the container goes down because during the restart the fresh container is recreated from the image.

As a result, we will need another tool to implement the storage. Such a tool is the volume.

So, what is a volume? From the technical point of view, volumes are basically directories on the node that runs the pod, which are mapped into the container filesystem. Also, volumes have an explicitly defined life cycle, which equals the pod life cycle. Whenever the pod is stopped, the volume is destroyed. On the other hand, when the containers inside the pod are restarted, the volume is unchanged; it just has to be remounted inside the container.

 Linux directory can also be a link to another directory or remote filesystem, such as **Network File System (NFS)**. As a result, removing the directory when the pod is stopped doesn't necessarily mean removing all the pieces of data. As a result, the way in which a volume behaves depends on its type—we will describe it in the next section.

OpenShift allows you to configure a number of volume types. Let's look at the most common of them.

Empty directory

Empty directory is, as its name suggests, an empty directory created in the node's filesystem. The directory is created when the pod is instantiated and is present as long as the pod runs on that node. When the pod is removed from the node for any reason, the directory is deleted.

The empty directory can be mounted inside any of the containers running inside the pod. An example usage for this kind of pod may be a directory shared between the containers that are used to gather common data.

 As we mentioned in the *Volumes* section, restarting any of the containers does not result in the deletion of the directory. The directory will be present till the pod exists and will be remounted inside a container that has a dependency on it after the container restart.

Host path

Host path is another type of persistent volume, which mounts the directory from the node's filesystem. In contrast to the empty directory, this kind of persistent volume does not create or destroy any new directories. For example, when a container needs access to some part of a configuration of the host, an administrator can mount the directory with this configuration inside the container filesystem.

Remote filesystems

As we hinted previously, a volume's directory doesn't have to point to the local filesystem. It can also point to remote filesystem directories. It is here that interesting stuff starts to happen. Let's look at it closer.

Quick recall here, when you use a remote filesystem, you have to create the storage on the server, export it, and then mount it on the client. On the client side, the mounting directory will be implemented as a remote filesystem client. As a result, operations on that directory will be propagated (using the given remote filesystem protocol) to the server.

OpenShift supports a number of remote filesystem protocols, for example, NFS, or Fiber Channel. Additionally, if you have knowledge of your cluster architecture, you can use proprietary remote filesystems, such as gcePersistentDisk (Google Cloud) or awsElasticBlockStore (Amazon Web Services).

Given the knowledge that we have, let's analyze the behavior of remote filesystems with OpenShift. When the pod with a remote filesystem volume is started, OpenShift creates a client directory on the node and mounts it inside the appropriate containers, according to the configuration. As usual, when containers are stopped, nothing happens to the directory, and it is remounted again when a container is restarted.

More interesting stuff happens when the pod is being removed or when the node crashes. In this scenario, the client directory is being deleted. Contrary to the empty directory scenario, this doesn't mean a loss of data. Deleting a client directory means that only one of the clients of the remote filesystem has been destroyed. The data inside the filesystem stays untouched.

As you can see, remote volumes enable us to create persistent storage, which can be mounted to our application. Also, the lifecycle is independent of the pods.

OK, we already know how volumes work and would gladly add them to our application. However, there is one problem, the configuration. The developer who would like to use one of those volumes has to have a lot of information on the cluster configuration: what kind of remote filesystem has been configured, or on which node it runs. More importantly, even if you gather such information from your administrator, you would need to ensure that it is configured correctly in each of your environments.

That's not good for a number of reasons. Firstly, we would like to decouple a developer from the cluster administrator. Ideally, the developer will specify the type of volume they need without needing to learn the details of the cluster configuration. Secondly, we emphasized in the preceding chapter the importance of a unified view of the cloud. Since this unified view is compromised now, you would have to reconfigure your pods for the testing environment to use NFS instead of Google disk. We clearly don't want that.

We need a tool that will solve those problems. Let's discuss **persistent volumes**.

PersistentVolume and PersistentVolumeClaims

Persistent volumes, similar to regular volumes, allow you to define different types of persistent storage. In fact, you can use persistent volumes to define storage types analogous to regular volumes, such as node directories or remote filesystems. Then, what is the difference?

Persistent volumes are Kubernetes objects, just as pods and services are objects. Their lifecycle is not related to any of the pods. In this context, we can think about persistent modules similar to the nodes—they are part of cluster infrastructure. Let's take a look at the sample `PersistentVolume`:

```
apiVersion: v1
kind: PersistentVolume
metadata:
//1
name: nfs
labels:
  zone: 5
//2
spec:
   capacity:
      storage: 100Mi
   accessModes:
   - ReadWriteMany
   nfs:
   server: 10.244.1.4
   path: "/exports"
```

As you can see in the preceding code, the `PersistentVolume` specifies the NFS server to which it is going to connect, in the same way as the volume. Compared to regular volume, it has a few additional fields: capacity, access mode, and metadata labels. You will learn in a moment why they are needed.

In the end, we would like to have this persistent storage mounted to our containers. How can we achieve that? We can do so using `PersistentVolumeClaims`. The `PersistentVolumeClaim` is an object that specifies the characteristics of the `PersistentVolume` that we need.

Let's look at the example again:

```
kind: PersistentVolumeClaim
apiVersion: v1
metadata:
  name: myclaim
spec:
  accessModes:
    - ReadWriteMany
  resources:
    requests:
      storage: 10Mi
  selector:
    matchLabels:
      zone: 5
```

As you can see in the preceding code, the `PersistentModule` claim specifies the amount of storage we need and the access type. As usual, in OpenShift, you are also able to use the label mechanism to provide additional match characteristics. In our example, we use those to specify from which zone the `PersistentVolume` should be taken.

 The `PersistentVolume` provides us with the capability of declaring persistent storage, which is a part of cluster infrastructure, and the `PersistentVolumeClaim` is a set of criteria that allows us to specify the `PersistentStorage` that we need.

However, how does the match process look and how does it actually relate to the pods that we are creating?

The `PersistentVolumeClaim` technically is a kind of a volume, and, as a result, you can refer to the given `PersistentVolumeClaim` from within your pod configuration. When the pod with such a claim is started, the `PersistentStorage` objects available in the system are evaluated. If a matching `PersistentVolume` can be found, it is mounted inside the containers that depend on that claim.

Let's take a look at the following example:

```
apiVersion: v1
metadata:
  name: mypod
spec:
  containers:
    - name: my-container
      image: tadamski/container
      volumeMounts:
      - mountPath: "/mount/storage1"
        name: pod
  volumes:
    - name: mypod
      persistentVolumeClaim:
        claimName: myclaim
```

As you can note, we were able to refer to the previously created `PersistentVolumeClaim` in our pod configuration. With this configuration, when `mypod` starts, `myclaim` would be evaluated, and if a matching `PersistentVolume` is found, it will be mounted inside `my-container`.

It's time to take a look at the bigger picture of the `PersistentVolume` and `PersistentVolumeClaims` architecture; those objects decouple storage provisioning from pod configuration. As a result, a developer is able to specify the characteristics of the storage that they need. They don't have to configure those volumes, and don't need to have the knowledge of the architecture of the given cluster. Also, the `PersistentVolume` is part of a cluster configuration, whereas the `PersistentVolumeClaim` is part of an application configuration; both can be created independently. The application that contains `PersistentVolumeClaim` objects can be created by a developer and deployed without changes in many OpenShift clusters. On the other hand, those clusters may contain different persistent storage configurations created by the administrators of those clusters. The details of those configurations are abstracted away from the developer.

The catalog-service with database

You have learned the essential knowledge to understand how to work with persistent storage in the OpenShift cloud. Now, let's take a look at this with a practical example. Let's update our **catalog-service** deployment so that it connects to the database.

Configuring PostgreSQL database

First, let's ensure that we have removed the previous version of the `catalog-service`. In order to do that, we will need to use the `oc` delete command. The command interface is the same as the interface for the get operation. You will be able to delete an object by directly specifying its name or use labels to indicate objects that you want to delete. There are many objects related to a single application, and we obviously don't want to delete them one by one. As a result, we will use the label version of the `delete` command for that:

```
oc delete all -l app=catalog-service
```

Now, we are ready to deploy the database. Open your web console and click on the **Add to the Project** button. We will search for the PostgreSQL project:

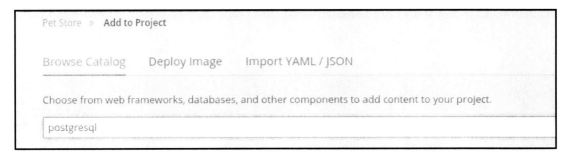

The search results in a number of options; we need to choose the data store option:

When you click on the **Select** button, the following form opens:

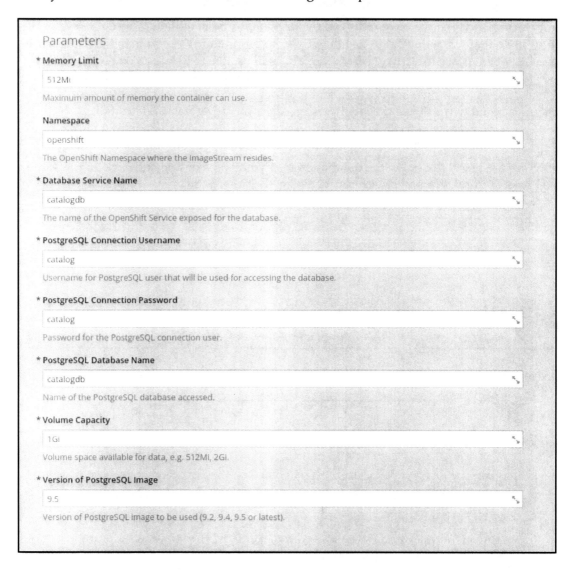

We changed the name of the database server and the name of the database instance to `catalogdb`. **For convenience purposes, we have set both the user and password to catalog.**

We will also override **Labels**:

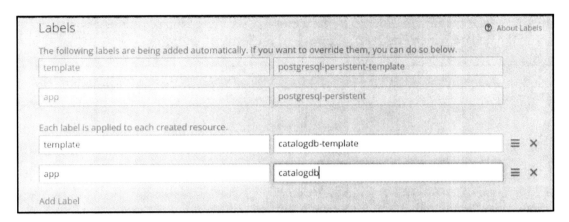

We will use a bunch of database containers for our different services. As a result, we can't use standard application and template labels. We change them to **catalogdb-template** and `catalogdb`.

After we have done that, we are ready to create an application; let's click on the **Create** button at the bottom of the page.

We have to wait for the moment till the pod has been started. Let's click on the **Overview page** button and further on **postgresql** deployment; we have to wait till there is one replica active:

The application is running. Let's fill our database with a number of pets so that we can test our service behavior. To do that we need to get access to the console of the container on which the database run. In order to achieve that we have to go to applications/pods menu, choose the pod on which PostgreSQL runs, and the terminal button:

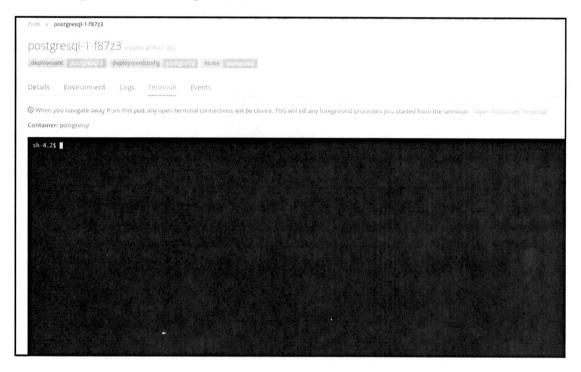

Let's fill the database now. Let's log into the user directory and create the SQL script there:

```
cd
vi items.sql
```

The script is very similar to the load scripts that we created in previous applications:

```
DROP TABLE IF EXISTS ITEM;

CREATE TABLE ITEM (id serial PRIMARY KEY, item_id varchar, name varchar,
description varchar, quantity smallint);

INSERT INTO ITEM(item_id, name, description, quantity) VALUES ('dbf67f4d-
f1c9-4fd4-96a8-65ee1a22b9ff', 'turtle', 'Slow friendly reptile. Let your
busy self see how it spends 100 years of his life laying on sand and
swimming.', 5);
```

```
INSERT INTO ITEM(item_id, name, description, quantity) VALUES
('fc7ee3ea-8f82-4144-bcc8-9a71f4d871bd', 'hamster', 'Energetic rodent –
great as a first pet. Will be your only inmate that takes his fitness
training serviously.', 10);
INSERT INTO ITEM(item_id, name, description, quantity) VALUES
('725dfad2-0b4d-455c-9385-b46c9f356e9b','goldfish', 'With its beauty it
will be the decoration of you aquarium. Likes gourmet fish feed and
postmodern poetry.', 3);
INSERT INTO ITEM(item_id, name, description, quantity) VALUES ('a2aa1ca7-
add8-4aae-b361-b7f92d82c3f5', 'lion', 'Loves playing the tag and cuddling
with other animals and people.', 9);
```

Please note, that we have changed the convention here. Instead of using names as item identifiers, we start using UIDs we will be the consistent ID for pets in the whole application.
Finally, we are going to execute the script:

```
psql -U catalog catalogdb < catalog.sql
```

The command above run PostgreSQL command line client. The -U parameter specifies the user (catalog in our example) and the catalogdb parameter specifies the schema on which the client must operate.

Our database is ready now and the question that comes to your mind may be: where are my persistent volumes? And the answer is: again OpenShift has done everything for you. Let's inspect it a little bit further.

Inspecting the volumes

In order to take a look at how the database is configured, let's use cli:

```
oc describe dc/catalogdb
```

You will be able to see that this deployment configuration has defined a volume of the PersistentVolumeClaim type:

```
Volumes:
 catalogdb-data:
  Type:       PersistentVolumeClaim (a reference to a PersistentVolumeClaim in the same namespace)
  ClaimName:  catalogdb
  ReadOnly:   false
```

Going further, let's analyze the `catalogdb` persistent volume claim:

```
oc describe pvc/catalogdb
```

We will be able to see that the claim has been created according to the database type that we provided and that it has been already bound:

```
Name:           catalogdb
Namespace:      petstore
StorageClass:
Status:         Bound
Volume:         pv0028
Labels:         app=catalogdb
                template=catalogdb-template
Annotations:    pv.kubernetes.io/bind-completed=yes
                pv.kubernetes.io/bound-by-controller=yes
Capacity:       100Gi
Access Modes:   RWO,ROX,RWX
Events:         <none>
```

As you see in the preceding screenshot, OpenShift has created a `PersitentVolumeClaim` based on information that you provided when an application was created from the template. The claim has been bound to one of the `PersitentVolumes` on the cluster. Since we are using Minishift now, the `PersitentVolumes` are implemented using disks inside the virtual machine. But we want to emphasize again that your application config wouldn't change an iota if you decided to deploy your application on any other OpenShift cluster.

Let's return to our example.

Updating catalog-service

We have to reconfigure our **catalog-service** again so that it works with the PostgreSQL database.

> **Examples refrence:** `chapter7/catalog-service-openshift-postgresql`.

Let's start with the `pom.xml` changes—we have to add Postgres dependency to it:

```
(...)

    <dependencies>
        (...)
        <dependency>
            <groupId>org.wildfly.swarm</groupId>
            <artifactId>jpa</artifactId>
            <version>${version.wildfly.swarm}</version>
        </dependency>
        <!-- 1 -->
        <dependency>
            <groupId>org.postgresql</groupId>
            <artifactId>postgresql</artifactId>
            <version>${version.postgresql}</version>
        </dependency>

    </dependencies>

(...)
```

We have changed the database driver from `h2` to `PostgreSQL` (1).

Let's change the datasource configuration:

```
swarm:
  datasources:
    data-sources:
      CatalogDS:
        driver-name: postgresql
        connection-url: jdbc:postgresql://catalogdb.petstore.svc/catalogdb
        user-name: catalog
      password: catalog
    jdbc-drivers:
      postgresql:
        driver-class-name: org.postgresql.Driver
        xa-datasource-name: org.postgresql.xa.PGXADataSource
        driver-module-name: org.postgresql.jdbc
```

We have to reconfigure the JDBC driver to user `postgresql` classes and reconfigure the datasource, so that it contains the data of our application. The meaning of catalogdb.petstore.svc address will be explained in the next chapter.

As in the previous database examples, we have to provide the `persistence` file:

```
<?xml version="1.0" encoding="UTF-8"?>
<persistence
        xmlns:xsi="http://www.w3.org/2001/XMLSchema-instance"
        version="2.1"
        xmlns="http://xmlns.jcp.org/xml/ns/persistence"
        xsi:schemaLocation="http://xmlns.jcp.org/xml/ns/persistence
http://xmlns.jcp.org/xml/ns/persistence/persistence_2_1.xsd">
    <persistence-unit name="CatalogPU" transaction-type="JTA">
        <jta-data-source>java:jboss/datasources/CatalogDS</jta-data-source>
    </persistence-unit>
</persistence>
```

Finally, we have to add the `postgreSQL` JDBC module to the application...

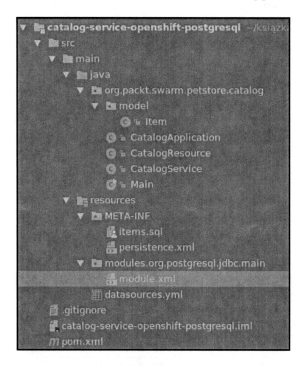

With the following contents:

```xml
<?xml version="1.0" encoding="UTF-8"?>
<module xmlns="urn:jboss:module:1.5" name="org.postgresql.jdbc">

  <resources>
    <artifact name="org.postgresql:postgresql:${version.postgresql}"/>
  </resources>
  <dependencies>
    <module name="javax.api"/>
    <module name="javax.transaction.api"/>
  </dependencies>
</module>
```

OK, now that we have reconfigured our **catalog-service**, it is time for interesting stuff. Let's deploy our application to OpenShift.

We will use the source-to-image build again as we did in the last chapter:

```
oc new-app wildflyswarm-10-
centos7~https://github.com/PacktPublishing/Hands-On-Cloud-Development-with-
WildFly.git --context-dir=chapter7/catalog-service-openshift-postgresql/ --
name=catalog-service
```

We have to wait till our fat-JAR has started. To verify that, we may take a look at the log of the pod on which the application was started:

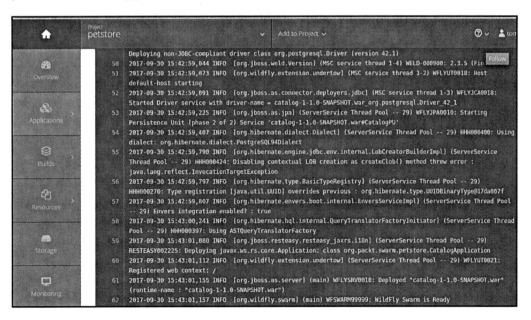

As in the preceding example, we have to create a route. After doing that, let's find out the address of **catalog-service** visible from outside the cluster:

Let's copy the route name and use `curl` to check whether we can get pet information using **catalog-service**:

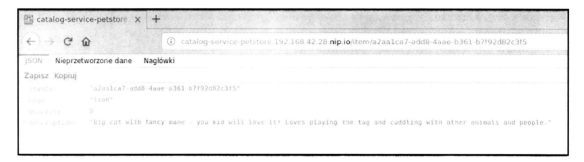

It works. Let's extend our service now so that it is able to persist data to the database.

Let's extend our `CatalogService`:

```
package org.packt.swarm.petstore.catalog;

import org.packt.swarm.petstore.catalog.model.Item;

import javax.enterprise.context.ApplicationScoped;
import javax.persistence.EntityManager;
import javax.persistence.PersistenceContext;
import javax.transaction.Transactional;
import java.util.List;
import java.util.UUID;
```

```
@ApplicationScoped
public class CatalogService {

    @PersistenceContext(unitName = "CatalogPU")
    private EntityManager em;

    public Item searchById(String itemId) {
        return em.createNamedQuery("Item.findById",
Item.class).setParameter("itemId", itemId).getSingleResult();
    }

    //1
    @Transactional
    public void add(Item item){
        //2
        item.setItemId(UUID.randomUUID().toString());
        em.persist(item);
    }

    //3
    public List<Item> getAll() {
        return em.createNamedQuery("Item.findAll",
Item.class).getResultList();
    }

}
```

We have extended the service with the add method (1). Note that the method is transactional and generates UUID for the items in the store (2). We have also added a method that lists all the items in the store (3). Note that we would need also to add NamedQuery for that:

```
(...)

@Entity
@Table(name = "item")
@NamedQueries({
        @NamedQuery(name="Item.findById",
                query="SELECT i FROM Item i WHERE i.itemId = :itemId"),
        @NamedQuery(name="Item.findAll",
                query="SELECT i FROM Item i")
})
public class Item {
(...)
```

We also have to add the POST method to the CatalogResource:

```java
package org.packt.swarm.petstore.catalog;

import org.packt.swarm.petstore.catalog.model.Item;

import javax.inject.Inject;
import javax.ws.rs.Consumes;
import javax.ws.rs.GET;
import javax.ws.rs.POST;
import javax.ws.rs.Path;
import javax.ws.rs.PathParam;
import javax.ws.rs.Produces;
import javax.ws.rs.core.MediaType;
import javax.ws.rs.core.Response;
import java.util.List;

@Path("/")
public class CatalogResource {

    @Inject
    private CatalogService catalogService;

    @GET
    @Path("item/{itemId}")
    @Produces(MediaType.APPLICATION_JSON)
    public Response searchById(@PathParam("itemId") String itemId) {
        try {
            Item item = catalogService.searchById(itemId);
            return Response.ok(item).build();
        } catch (Exception e) {
            e.printStackTrace();
            return
Response.status(Response.Status.BAD_REQUEST).entity(e.getMessage()).build()
;
        }
    }

    //1
    @POST
    @Path("item")
    //2
    @Produces(MediaType.APPLICATION_JSON)
    //3
    @Consumes(MediaType.APPLICATION_JSON)
    public Response addNew(Item item) {
        try {
```

```
            catalogService.add(item);
            return Response.ok(item).build();
        } catch (Exception e) {
            return
Response.status(Response.Status.BAD_REQUEST).entity(e.getMessage()).build()
;
        }
    }


    //2
    @GET
    @Path("item")
    @Produces(MediaType.APPLICATION_JSON)
    @Consumes(MediaType.APPLICATION_JSON)
    public Response getAll() {
        try {
            List<Item> item = catalogService.getAll();
            return Response.ok(item).build();
        } catch (Exception e) {
            return
Response.status(Response.Status.BAD_REQUEST).entity(e.getMessage()).build()
;
        }
    }


}
```

We have implemented the addNew method, which uses the CatalogService instance to add an Item object(1) to the database. As you will have noticed in the preceding code, both the Request parameter and Response are JSON objects. They are parsed automatically by a server; the only thing that we must do is annotate the method with the @Produces (2) and @Consumes (3) annotations. In the method, we use the catalogService to store a given Item object. Finally, we return either the ok response (5) or an error response (6) based on the result of the store operation.

We have also implemented getAll method which will allow us to request information about all the pets in the store (2).

After the application is ready, you have to commit the changed files and push them to GitHub. When you do this, you can enter the web console and trigger the build of the updated service. In order to do it, you have to click on **Build | Build in the Webconsole**, select the **catalog-service**, and click on the **Start Build** button in the top-right corner:

After the application starts, we have to wait till it has been deployed in the cloud. Let's use `curl` to `POST` new Item in our store:

```
[tomek@localhost ~]$ curl -H "Content-Type: application/json" -X POST -d '{"name":"rabbit","description":"Small m
ammal which jumps a lot","quantity":"7"}' http://catalog-service-petstore.192.168.42.48.nip.io/item; echo
{"itemId":"059e4b9a-7f2f-46f8-8653-0134178762e1","name":"rabbit","quantity":7,"description":"Small mammal which j
umps a lot"}
[tomek@localhost ~]$ 
```

Everything seems fine, so let's check what items are available in the store using the request that we have just implemented:

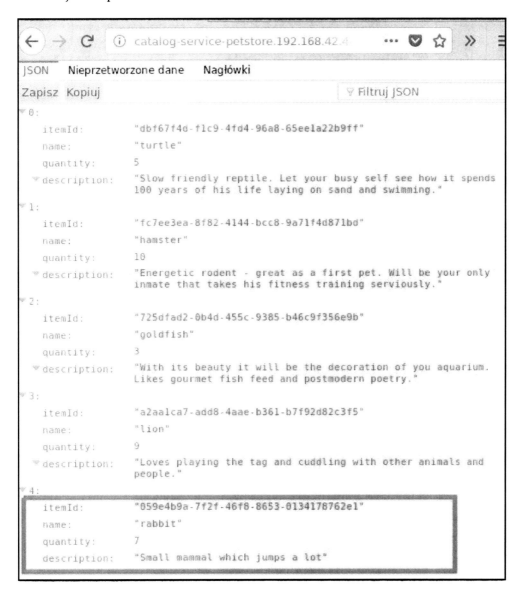

There are three rabbits in our database. Our service is working correctly inside the OpenShift cluster.

We may now check that the storage is indeed persistent. Let's get into the web console and terminate both catalog-service and database pods. In order to do that, enter web console, click **Applications | Pods** and choose the **database** pod. Later click on **Actions** in the right, upper corner and choose **Delete**. Repeat those actions for **catalog-service** pod. After both pods have been restarted (you can monitor that in **Applications | Pods** view), you can again list all items. You should be able to see extract the same result as on the preceding screenshot.

Summary

In this chapter, you learned how to configure persistence for the services deployed in OpenShift.

This chapter started with theoretical knowledge, giving you more details on volumes and their different types. Later, you learned a particularly useful type of the volume the `PersistentVolumeClaim`. You also learned why it is necessary, how it is related to the `PersistentVolume`, and how to use it.

Finally, we extended your `catalogService` so that it uses the `postgresql` database as the storage.

8
Scaling and Connecting Your Services

In this chapter, we will look in greater detail at the process of deploying, scaling, and connecting your applications. In `Chapter 6`, *Deploying Applications on the Cloud with OpenShift*, you have already learned the basic information about deploying services to the OpenShift cloud. Now it's time to extend this knowledge and learn how to use it in practice.

Let's start with deployments.

Deployments

Let's examine what happens under the hood during deployment of our services. We are going to continue work on an example from the previous chapter.

Examples reference: `chapter8/catalog-service-openshift-load-balancing`.

You have to open the web console, and navigate to **Applications| Deployments | catalog-service**:

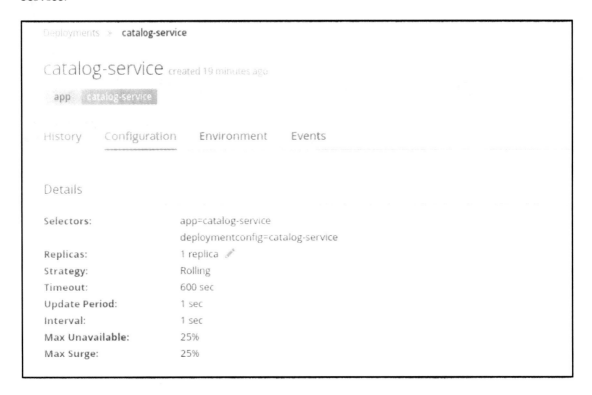

Now we will be able to see the deployment configuration. This is the graphical representation of OpenShift's `DeploymentConfiguration` object.

As you learned in `Chapter 6`, *Deploying Applications on the Cloud with OpenShift*, OpenShift adds another layer on top of Kubernetes to provide a more convenient and productive programmer experience. It does that, among other things, by extending the object model of Kubernetes. `DeploymentConfiguration` and **Deployments** are OpenShift objects that extend the Kubernetes object model.

The `DeploymentConfiguration` object manages the creation of the **Deployments** objects. It contains all the necessary information to create **Deployments**, which, as its name suggests, represents an instance of deployment. When one of the Deployments triggers happens, the old deployment object is replaced by the new one. All of the deployment objects are based on `DeploymentConfiguration`. **Deployments**, among others, encapsulate Kubernetes's `ReplicationController` object. Let's understand it in greater detail.

Learning the basics of ReplicationController

`ReplicationController` contains the following information: the pod template, selector, and the number of replicas. Let's examine those further.

The pod template is basically a pod definition. It contains information about the containers, volumes, ports, and labels. Every pod created by this replication controller will be started using this pod template. The selector is used to determine which pods are governed by this `ReplicationController`. Finally, the number of replicas is the number of pods that we want to be running.

Kubernetes works in the following way: it monitors the current state of the cluster, and if that state is different from the desired state it takes actions so that the desired state is restored. The same thing happens with `ReplicationControllers`. `ReplicationController` continuously monitors the number of pods that are associated with it. If the number of the pods is different than the desired number, it starts or stops pods so that the desired state is restored. The pod is started using the pod template.

Let's examine the `ReplicationController` that Kubernetes created for our catalog-service. To do this, we will use the CLI:

```
[tomek@localhost ~]$ oc get replicationcontrollers -l app=catalog-service
NAME                DESIRED    CURRENT    READY    AGE
catalog-service-1   0          0          0        21m
catalog-service-2   0          0          0        5m
catalog-service-3   1          1          1        5m
[tomek@localhost ~]$
```

As you will notice in the preceding screenshot, there are three replication controllers created for **catalog-service**. This is the case because of each redeployment of the application results in the creation of a new deployment object with its own replication controller. Note that only **catalog-service-3** has the desired number of instances greater than 0—the previous deployments have been made inactive when the new deployment was taking place.

Let's take a look at the description of the active controller:

```
[tomek@localhost ~]$ oc describe replicationcontroller/catalog-service-3
Name:          catalog-service-3
Namespace:     petstore
Selector:      app=catalog-service,deployment=catalog-service-3,deploymentconfig=catalog-service
Labels:        app=catalog-service
               openshift.io/deployment-config.name=catalog-service
Annotations:   openshift.io/deployer-pod.name=catalog-service-3-deploy
               openshift.io/deployment-config.latest-version=3
               openshift.io/deployment-config.name=catalog-service
               openshift.io/deployment.phase=Complete
               openshift.io/deployment.replicas=
               openshift.io/deployment.status-reason=manual change
               openshift.io/encoded-deployment-config={"kind":"DeploymentConfig","apiVersion":"v1","metadata":{"name":"catalog-service"
,"namespace":"petstore","selfLink":"/apis/apps.openshift.io/v1/namespaces/petsto...
Replicas:      1 current / 1 desired
Pods Status:   1 Running / 0 Waiting / 0 Succeeded / 0 Failed
Pod Template:
  Labels:      app=catalog-service
               deployment=catalog-service-3
               deploymentconfig=catalog-service
  Annotations: openshift.io/deployment-config.latest-version=3
               openshift.io/deployment-config.name=catalog-service
               openshift.io/deployment.name=catalog-service-3
               openshift.io/generated-by=OpenShiftWebConsole
  Containers:
   catalog-service:
    Image:     tadamski/catalog-service@sha256:b40765874ca3adb7f7d2fb06b8a8b10a9ebc485f6fd9ee502c05070e0984fe55
    Ports:     8080/TCP, 8778/TCP, 9779/TCP
    Environment:
      POSTGRESQL_HOST:       172.30.199.153
      POSTGRESQL_USER:       petstore
      POSTGRESQL_PASSWORD:   XyIpmjEWlXCQnPsG
      POSTGRESQL_SCHEMA:     petstoredb
    Mounts:    <none>
  Volumes:     <none>
Events:
  FirstSeen   LastSeen    Count   From                    SubObjectPath   Type        Reason              Message
  ---------   --------    -----   ----                    -------------   ----        ------              -------
  12m         12m         1       replication-controller                  Normal      SuccessfulCreate    Created pod: cat
alog-service-3-3kr44
```

The selector has three labels: app, deployment, and deployment-config. It unambiguously
identifies the pods associated with the given deployment.

> Exactly the same labels are used in the pod template. Other parts of the
> pod template contain the image from which the container is built, and the
> environment variables that we provided during the creation of the service.
> Finally, the number of current and desired replicas is set, by default, to
> one.

OK. So how do we scale our service so that it runs on more than one instance? Let's move to the web console again. We need to navigate to **Application** | **Deployments** again and enter the **catalog-service** configuration:

To scale the **catalog-service** application, we have to adjust the **Replicas** field to the number of instances that we want to have. That's it.

When we look at the `ReplicationControllers` in the `oc`, we will see the following information:

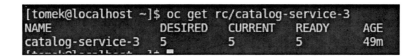

The number of pods has been changed to **5**. As we saw in the oc output, additional pods have been started and we now have five instances. Let's check in the console (navigate to **Applications | Pods**):

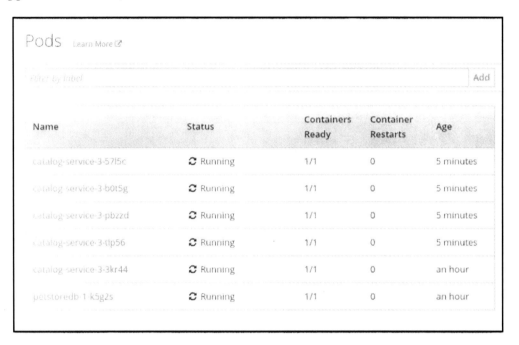

OpenShift has indeed scaled our application according to our needs.

After having worked with OpenShift for some time, you should be able to see what we meant in Chapter 6, *Deploying Applications on the Cloud with OpenShift*, when we wrote that OpenShift builds an effective and easy-to-use application development environment on top of Kubernetes. The preceding example showed how it works very well: Kubernetes is responsible for making sure that the state of the cluster equals the description provided. In the preceding example, this description is provided by a ReplicationController object (which is part of the Kubernetes object model). Note, however, that OpenShift has abstracted away all the nitty-gritty details from us. We have only provided the information such as the address of the code repository or number of replicas that we want to have. The OpenShift layer abstracts away the technical details of cluster configuration and provides us with convenient, easy-to-use tools, which allow the programmer to concentrate on the development.

Let's return to our main topic. The next thing that we will configure is **load balancing**.

Load balancing

We have just learned how to scale our service. The next natural step is to configure the load balancer. The good news is that OpenShift will do most of the stuff automatically for us.

In Chapter 6, *Deploying Applications on the Cloud with OpenShift*, where we introduced services, we learned that a service is reached using a virtual cluster IP. To understand how load balancing works, let's understand how cluster IP is implemented.

As we have also learned here, each node in a Kubernetes cluster runs a bunch of services, which allow a cluster to provide its functionality. One of those services is **kube-proxy**. Kube-proxy runs on every node and is, among other things, responsible for service implementation. Kube-proxy continuously monitors the object model describing the cluster and gathers information about currently active services and pods on which those services run. When the new service appears, kube-proxy modifies the iptables rules so that the virtual cluster's IP is routed to one of the available pods. The iptables rules are created so that the choice of the pod is random. Also, note that those IP rules have to be constantly rewritten to match the current state of the cluster.

A kube-proxy runs on every node of the cluster. Owing to that, on each node, there is a set of iptables rules, which forward the package to the appropriate pods. As a result, the service is accessible from each node of the cluster on its virtual cluster IP.

What's the implication of that from the client service perspective? The cluster infrastructure is hidden from the service client. The client doesn't need to have any knowledge about nodes, pods, and their dynamic movement inside the cluster. They just invoke the service using its IP as if it was a physical host.

Let's return to our example and look at the load balancing of our host. Let's return to the example in which we are working within this chapter. We statically scaled our catalog service to five instances. Let's enter the web console in order to look at all the pods on which the application currently runs:

Let's trace to which pods are the requests forwarded. In order to achieve that, we implemented a simple REST filter:

```
package org.packt.swarm.petstore.catalog;

import javax.ws.rs.container.ContainerResponseFilter;
import javax.ws.rs.container.ContainerRequestContext;
import javax.ws.rs.container.ContainerResponseContext;
import javax.ws.rs.ext.Provider;
import java.io.IOException;

//1
@Provider
public class PodNameResponseFilter implements ContainerResponseFilter {
    public void filter(ContainerRequestContext req,
ContainerResponseContext res)
            throws IOException
    {
        //2
        res.getHeaders().add("pod", System.getenv("HOSTNAME"));
    }
}
```

The preceding filter adds a `"pod"` property to the response headers. The filter will be evaluated after the response is processed (1). On each pod, there is a `"HOSTNAME"` environment variable set. We can use this variable and add it to the response metadata (2).

As a result, we are ready to trace the load balancing:

```
[tomek@localhost ~]$ curl -I http://catalog-service-petstore.192.168.42.48.nip.io/
item/fc7ee3ea-8f82-4144-bcc8-9a71f4d871bd
HTTP/1.1 200 OK
pod: catalog-service-1-8842l
Content-Type: application/json
Content-Length: 206
Date: Sun, 18 Mar 2018 13:37:00 GMT
Set-Cookie: 143a3872a836a2875d0e32fb7af4450c=a096c3835f5eb25fa681fcc839e114f0; pat
h=/; HttpOnly
Cache-control: private

[tomek@localhost ~]$ curl -I http://catalog-service-petstore.192.168.42.48.nip.io/
item/fc7ee3ea-8f82-4144-bcc8-9a71f4d871bd
HTTP/1.1 200 OK
pod: catalog-service-1-sq05t
Content-Type: application/json
Content-Length: 206
Date: Sun, 18 Mar 2018 13:37:07 GMT
Set-Cookie: 143a3872a836a2875d0e32fb7af4450c=246506eedb4cfc092f2862ddf4df4fc9; pat
h=/; HttpOnly
Cache-control: private

[tomek@localhost ~]$ curl -I http://catalog-service-petstore.192.168.42.48.nip.io/
item/fc7ee3ea-8f82-4144-bcc8-9a71f4d871bd
HTTP/1.1 200 OK
pod: catalog-service-1-zlb85
Content-Type: application/json
Content-Length: 206
Date: Sun, 18 Mar 2018 13:37:10 GMT
Set-Cookie: 143a3872a836a2875d0e32fb7af4450c=c511a0b6fb50bac9bfb43165db52909d; pat
h=/; HttpOnly
Cache-control: private

[tomek@localhost ~]$ curl -I http://catalog-service-petstore.192.168.42.48.nip.io/
item/fc7ee3ea-8f82-4144-bcc8-9a71f4d871bd
HTTP/1.1 200 OK
pod: catalog-service-1-rcd42
Content-Type: application/json
Content-Length: 206
Date: Sun, 18 Mar 2018 13:37:11 GMT
Set-Cookie: 143a3872a836a2875d0e32fb7af4450c=3b42672ae622d5ba049a797c69e2ecc8; pat
h=/; HttpOnly
Cache-control: private

[tomek@localhost ~]$ curl -I http://catalog-service-petstore.192.168.42.48.nip.io/
item/fc7ee3ea-8f82-4144-bcc8-9a71f4d871bd
HTTP/1.1 200 OK
pod: catalog-service-1-qznz9
Content-Type: application/json
Content-Length: 206
Date: Sun, 18 Mar 2018 13:37:12 GMT
Set-Cookie: 143a3872a836a2875d0e32fb7af4450c=15303f0b3403ed17f9d3790998eb63da; pat
h=/; HttpOnly
Cache-control: private

[tomek@localhost ~]$
```

In the preceding screenshot, note that the request is being automatically load balanced among the available pods.

Service discovery

We have already shown you how to configure balancing for our application. We know now that you have access to the virtual cluster IP address behind which the request is being balanced by OpenShift. However, how do we actually know how to connect to our services? We are going to learn that in the next topic. Before we do that, we must introduce our new services that will be talking to each other.

New services

In the first chapter, we briefly introduced the pet store application and described the services that constitute it. By now, we have used solely the catalog service in our examples. Now it's time to implement both the pricing service and customer gateway service. These services will serve as an example in this and the future chapters. Let's start with the pricing service.

The pricing service

The pricing service is very similar to catalog service. It can be used to obtain prices for a pet using their names. Let's go straight to the implementation. Initially, we have to create the database. As before, we will use the PostgreSQL template:

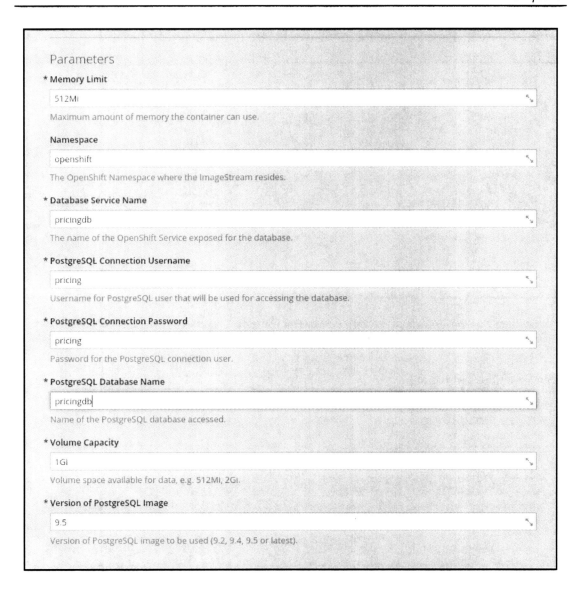

As with the catalog service's database, we would also like to override the labels:

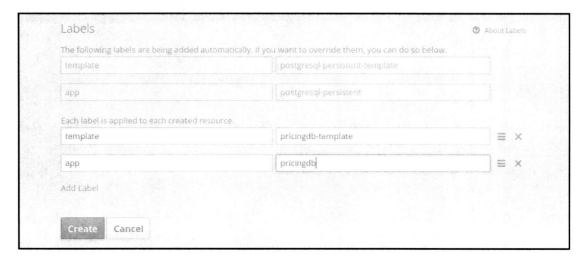

To populate the database, we have to create the following script:

```
vi pets.sql
```

Now, enter the sample data:

```
DROP TABLE IF EXISTS PRICE;
CREATE TABLE PRICE (id serial PRIMARY KEY, item_id varchar, price
smallint);
INSERT INTO PRICE(item_id, price) VALUES ('dbf67f4d-
f1c9-4fd4-96a8-65ee1a22b9ff', 50);
INSERT INTO PRICE(item_id, price) VALUES ('fc7ee3ea-8f82-4144-
bcc8-9a71f4d871bd', 30);
INSERT INTO PRICE(item_id, price) VALUES ('725dfad2-0b4d-455c-9385-
b46c9f356e9b', 15);
INSERT INTO PRICE(item_id, price) VALUES ('a2aa1ca7-add8-4aae-b361-
b7f92d82c3f5', 3000);
```

To populate the database, we will execute the following script:

```
psql -U pricing pricingdb < pets.sql
```

Our pricing database is ready. We can now start writing the code.

Examples reference: chapter8/pricing-service.

We have to configure the database in the similar way that we did for **catalog-service**.

```
swarm:
  datasources:
    data-sources:
      PricingDS:
        driver-name: postgresql
        connection-url: jdbc:postgresql://pricingdb.petstore.svc/pricingdb
        user-name: pricing
        password: pricing
    jdbc-drivers:
      postgresql:
        driver-class-name: org.postgresql.Driver
        xa-datasource-name: org.postgresql.xa.PGXADataSource
        driver-module-name: org.postgresql.jdbc
```

In order for the database to work, we have to provide the JDBC driver module:

As you can see, we also need persistence.xml:

```
<?xml version="1.0" encoding="UTF-8"?>
<persistence
        xmlns:xsi="http://www.w3.org/2001/XMLSchema-instance"
        version="2.1"
        xmlns="http://xmlns.jcp.org/xml/ns/persistence"
        xsi:schemaLocation="http://xmlns.jcp.org/xml/ns/persistence
http://xmlns.jcp.org/xml/ns/persistence/persistence_2_1.xsd">
    <persistence-unit name="PricingPU" transaction-type="JTA">
        <jta-data-source>java:jboss/datasources/PricingDS</jta-data-source>
    </persistence-unit>
</persistence>
```

We have to provide an Entity:

```
package org.packt.swarm.petstore.pricing;

import com.fasterxml.jackson.annotation.JsonIgnore;

import javax.persistence.Column;
import javax.persistence.Entity;
import javax.persistence.GeneratedValue;
import javax.persistence.GenerationType;
import javax.persistence.Id;
import javax.persistence.NamedQueries;
import javax.persistence.NamedQuery;
import javax.persistence.SequenceGenerator;
import javax.persistence.Table;

//1
@Entity
//2
@Table(name = "Price")
//3
@NamedQueries({
        @NamedQuery(name="Price.findByName",
                query="SELECT p FROM Price p WHERE p.name = :name"),
})
public class Price {

    //4
    @Id
    @GeneratedValue(strategy = GenerationType.SEQUENCE, generator =
"price_sequence")
    @SequenceGenerator(name = "price_sequence", sequenceName =
"price_id_seq")
    //5
    @JsonIgnore
    private int id;

    //6
    @Column(length = 30)
    private String name;
    @Column
    private int price;

    public int getId() {
        return id;
    }
```

```
    public void setId(int id) {
        this.id = id;
    }

    public String getName() {
        return name;
    }

    public void setName(String name) {
        this.name = name;
    }


    public int getPrice() {
        return price;
    }

    public void setPrice(int price) {
        this.price = price;
    }
}
```

In the preceding snippet, we have created a JPA entity (1), which references the `"Price"` table that we have just created (2). We have provided `NamedQueries`, which will enable us to search the price of a pet by a name (3). An `id`, as in `catalogdb`, is generated using the Postgres sequence (4) and is not parsed in the JSON response (5). Finally, we have annotated the fields mapped to the `price` and `name` columns (6).

As in `catalog-service`, we will need a service:

```
package org.packt.swarm.petstore.pricing;

import org.packt.swarm.petstore.pricing.model.Price;

import javax.enterprise.context.ApplicationScoped;
import javax.persistence.EntityManager;
import javax.persistence.PersistenceContext;
import javax.ws.rs.WebApplicationException;
import java.util.List;

@ApplicationScoped
public class PricingService {

    @PersistenceContext(unitName = "PricingPU")
    private EntityManager em;

    public Price findByItemId(String itemId) {
```

```
            return em.createNamedQuery("Price.findByItemId",
    Price.class).setParameter("itemId", itemId).getSingleResult();
        }
    }
```

We also need REST resource:

```java
package org.packt.swarm.petstore.pricing;

import org.packt.swarm.petstore.pricing.model.Price;

import javax.inject.Inject;
import javax.ws.rs.GET;
import javax.ws.rs.Path;
import javax.ws.rs.PathParam;
import javax.ws.rs.Produces;
import javax.ws.rs.core.Context;
import javax.ws.rs.core.MediaType;
import javax.ws.rs.core.Response;
import javax.ws.rs.core.SecurityContext;

@Path("/")
public class PricingResource {

    @Inject
    private PricingService pricingService;

    @GET
    @Path("price/{item_id}")
    @Produces(MediaType.APPLICATION_JSON)
    public Response priceByName(@PathParam("item_id") String itemId) {
        Price result = pricingService.findByItemId(itemId);
        return Response.ok(result).build();
    }
}
```

We would also need an application:

```java
package org.packt.swarm.petstore.pricing;

import javax.ws.rs.ApplicationPath;
import javax.ws.rs.core.Application;

@ApplicationPath("/")
public class PricingApplication extends Application {
}
```

Our second service is ready. It's time to deploy it on OpenShift. Push your application to your GitHub repository and invoke:

```
oc new-app wildflyswarm-10-
centos7~https://github.com/PacktPublishing/Hands-On-Cloud-Development-with-
WildFly.git --context-dir=chapter8/pricing-service --name=pricing-service
```

After your application is deployed, you can create a route to it and verify that it indeed works:

It indeed does. Let's move to the second service.

The customer gateway service

In this section, the stuff becomes more interesting again. The customer-gateway service is a gateway to our application, which would provide the external interface for the web client. The first request that we will implement is obtaining the list of pets. Let's take a look at the following diagram:

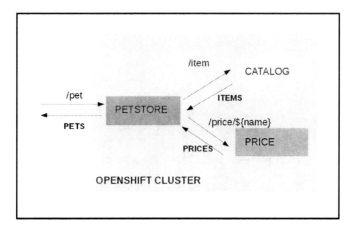

When the `/catalog/item` request is being executed, the service asks **CATALOG** for available items. Based on that information, the pet store service asks the **PRICE** service about the price of each pet, merges the results, and then returns them to the client. However, how will the gateway service know the addresses of the services? We will find that out soon.

Examples reference: `chapter8/customer-gateway-env`.

The customer service is configured in a similar way to previous services. If you have doubts regarding some parts of configuration please refer to the description of those.

Let's look at the implementation details of `catalog/item` request starting with the REST resource:

```
package org.packt.swarm.petstore;

import org.packt.swarm.petstore.api.CatalogItemView;

import javax.inject.Inject;
import javax.ws.rs.GET;
import javax.ws.rs.Path;
import javax.ws.rs.Produces;
import javax.ws.rs.core.MediaType;
import javax.ws.rs.core.Response;
import java.util.List;

@Path("/")
public class GatewayResource {

    @Inject
    private GatewayService gatewayService;

    //1
    @GET
    @Path("/catalog/item")
    @Produces(MediaType.APPLICATION_JSON)
    public Response getItems() {
        //2
        List<CatalogItemView> result = gatewayService.getItems();
        return Response.ok(result).build();
    }
```

The `getItems` method gathers the items from the `CatalogService` (1), obtains a price for all of them, and merges the obtained results into the list of pets available in the store. Please note that we have introduced `CatalogItemView`—a transport object which is a part of the API for the web client.

We have also implemented the service:

```
package org.packt.swarm.petstore;

import org.packt.swarm.petstore.api.CatalogItemView;
import org.packt.swarm.petstore.catalog.api.CatalogItem;
import org.packt.swarm.petstore.pricing.api.Price;
import org.packt.swarm.petstore.proxy.CatalogProxy;
import org.packt.swarm.petstore.proxy.PricingProxy;

import javax.enterprise.context.ApplicationScoped;
import javax.inject.Inject;
import java.util.ArrayList;
import java.util.List;

@ApplicationScoped
public class GatewayService {

    //2
    @Inject
    private CatalogProxy catalogProxy;

    @Inject
    private PricingProxy pricingProxy;


    //1
    public List<CatalogItemView> getItems() {
        List<CatalogItemView> views = new ArrayList<>();
        for(CatalogItem item: catalogProxy.getAllItems()) {
            Price price = pricingProxy.getPrice(item.getItemId());

            CatalogItemView view = new CatalogItemView();
            view.setItemId(item.getItemId());
            view.setName(item.getName());
            view.setPrice(price.getPrice());
            view.setQuantity(item.getQuantity());
            view.setDescription(item.getDescription());
```

```
            views.add(view);
        }
        return views;
    }

}
```

The getItems method implementation (1) is pretty straightforward. We are combining data from catalog and pricing services and returning the list of resulting object. The most interesting part here is the proxies which enable us to communicate with those services (2). Let's learn how to implement them.

Environment variables

When the new service is created, its coordinates are written into environment variables in every pod in the cluster.

Let's log in to one of the pods inside the cluster and take a look at it. All the OpenShift environment variable names are written in uppercase, and we need the data about the pricing service:

```
sh-4.2$ env | grep PRICING SERVICE
PRICING_SERVICE_PORT=tcp://172.30.104.212:8080
PRICING_SERVICE_PORT_8778_TCP=tcp://172.30.104.212:8778
PRICING_SERVICE_PORT_9779_TCP_ADDR=172.30.104.212
PRICING_SERVICE_SERVICE_PORT_8778_TCP=8778
PRICING_SERVICE_PORT_8080_TCP_ADDR=172.30.104.212
PRICING_SERVICE_PORT_8778_TCP_ADDR=172.30.104.212
PRICING_SERVICE_PORT_8080_TCP=tcp://172.30.104.212:8080
PRICING_SERVICE_PORT_9779_TCP_PROTO=tcp
PRICING_SERVICE_PORT_8778_TCP_PORT=8778
PRICING_SERVICE_SERVICE_PORT_9779_TCP=9779
PRICING_SERVICE_PORT_8080_TCP_PROTO=tcp
PRICING_SERVICE_SERVICE_PORT_8080_TCP=8080
PRICING_SERVICE_PORT_8778_TCP_PROTO=tcp
PRICING_SERVICE_PORT_8080_TCP_PORT=8080
PRICING_SERVICE_SERVICE_HOST=172.30.104.212
PRICING_SERVICE_PORT_9779_TCP_PORT=9779
PRICING_SERVICE_SERVICE_PORT=8080
PRICING_SERVICE_PORT_9779_TCP=tcp://172.30.104.212:9779
```

In the preceding screenshot, note that there are a number of variables describing the coordinates of the service. The property that interests us is the host address:

```
PRICING_SERVICE_SERVICE_HOST=172.30.104.212
```

Note that this is the virtual cluster IP again. As a result, as long as the service is not removed, the proxy address will stay the same. Underlying infrastructure changes caused by deployments, node addition, or failures will not result in the change of the previous address.

Let's write proxies that will use this variable in order to connect to the services. We will start with the pricing-service proxy:

```
package org.packt.swarm.petstore.proxy;

import org.packt.swarm.petstore.pricing.api.Price;

import javax.enterprise.context.ApplicationScoped;
import javax.ws.rs.client.Client;
import javax.ws.rs.client.ClientBuilder;
import javax.ws.rs.client.WebTarget;
import javax.ws.rs.core.MediaType;

@ApplicationScoped
public class PricingProxy {

    private String targetPath;

    PricingProxy(){
        //1
        targetPath = "http://" +
System.getenv("PRICING_SERVICE_SERVICE_HOST")+":"+8080;
    }

    public Price getPrice(String name){
        //2
        Client client = ClientBuilder.newClient();
        WebTarget target = client.target(targetPath +"/price/" + name);
        return target.request(MediaType.APPLICATION_JSON).get(Price.class);
    }
}
```

That's just it. We obtained the clusterIP of the pricing-service when the proxy was being created (1) and the user straightforward REST Client API to provide an adapter for the getPrice method invocation (2).

The implementation of catalogProxy is analogous.

Now we are ready to check whether our application is working. Let's create a route for the `petstore` service and check the web browser:

It works indeed. This solution has a major disadvantage though—an ordering problem. If the pod is created before the service, then service coordinates won't be present in the pod environment. Is there a better way to discover the services, then? Yes, through **Domain Name Service (DNS)**.

DNS discovery

Each OpenShift cluster contains a DNS service. This service allows you to discover services easily using the service name. Each service registers to the DNS service during the registration, and later periodically sends live messages to it. The DNS server creates a record using the following pattern:

```
${service name}.${application name}.svc
```

Let's take the pricing service as an example. We have created the `petstore` application. As a result, the name of the service created using the preceding pattern would be pricing-service.petstore.svc.

We can confirm that information inside web console. Let's navigate to **Applications |**
Services | pricing-service:

Take note of the `hostname` field—this is the address that we created previously. Another important thing to note is that those service names are visible only from inside the cluster.

We are now ready to refactor our application to use elegant DNS discovery.

 Examples reference: `chapter8/customer-gateway-dns`.

We have to rewrite both our proxies. Let's start with `PricingProxy`:

```java
package org.packt.swarm.petstore.proxy;

import org.packt.swarm.petstore.pricing.api.Price;

import javax.enterprise.context.ApplicationScoped;
import javax.ws.rs.client.Client;
import javax.ws.rs.client.ClientBuilder;
import javax.ws.rs.client.WebTarget;
import javax.ws.rs.core.MediaType;

@ApplicationScoped
public class PricingProxy {

    //1
    private final String targetPath =
System.getProperty("proxy.pricing.url");

    public Price getPrice(String itemId){
        Client client = ClientBuilder.newClient();
        WebTarget target = client.target(targetPath + "/price/" + itemId);
        return target.request(MediaType.APPLICATION_JSON).get(Price.class);
    }
}
```

We defined a `targetPath` that we can use repeatedly to connect to services (1). We are going to provide it as a parameter using YAML configuration:

```yaml
proxy:
  catalog:
    url: "http://catalog-service.petstore.svc:8080"
  pricing:
    url: "http://pricing-service.petstore.svc:8080"
```

Again, `CatalogProxy` implementation is analogous.

Now we are ready to redeploy the customer-gateway service again. You can once again check whether it works correctly.

As you may recall, we were using the name of the service when we were creating the environment file for our databases. Each service in the cluster can be reached using this method.

Summary

In this chapter, you learned how to scale and discover services inside the cluster. As you were able to see throughout this chapter, most of the work was done by OpenShift. Load balancing is implemented automatically by the services, and the integrated DNS service allows for straightforward service discovery.

In the next chapter, you will learn more about networking. You will also learn how to provide resiliency to a service invocation so that underlying network failures won't cause your application to stop working.

9
Configuring Continuous Integration Using Jenkins

In this chapter, we will teach you how to integrate the pet store application with Jenkins, a **Continuous Integration** (CI) server. We will introduce CI concepts and how they can be implemented using Jenkins. We will configure a sample `pipeline` so that you can see how changes in application code are propagated to the deployed application.

Let's start with the builds.

Learning OpenShift builds

In the previous chapters, we did some serious magic in order to build our application. To be able to run the builds, we executed the following command:

```
oc create -f
https://raw.githubusercontent.com/wildfly-swarm/sti-wildflyswarm/master/1.0
/wildflyswarm-sti-all.json
```

In previous chapters, when we wanted to build our application, we invoked the following command:

```
oc new-app wildflyswarm-10-
centos7~https://github.com/PacktPublishing/Hands-On-Cloud-Development-with-
WildFly.git (...)
```

After a lot of mysterious stuff had happened (as indicated by growing logs), we were able to see our application working. Now, it's time to explain what actually happened under the hood. Let's get to know OpenShift builds.

In general, an OpenShift build is an operation that transforms input parameters into a resulting object that is used to start an application. In most cases, the build will transform the source code into an image that will be later deployed on the cluster.

The details of the build process operation depend on the build type (about which we will learn in a moment), but the general algorithm looks as follows:

1. The build container starts from the build image
2. Sources from all the inputs are being injected into the container
3. The build scripts are being run
4. The output docker image is created

The new concept that is being introduced here is the build container. Let's take a look at it a little bit closer. What actually is its purpose? The container in which you are building your application has to contain all the libraries, tools, and runtimes that are necessary to build and run your application. For example, if you use the WildFly AS builder image, it will contain Java, Maven, and WildFly runtimes among others. After the application is built, the same image is used as a base for the Docker image that will be deployed to OpenShift. Speaking precisely, your application will be added as another layer on top of the builder image, resulting in a runnable image with your application. The good news here is that although you can easily create an image yourself, in most cases those images will be created by the tool provider.

The input types can be provided from any resources, such as GitHub repositories, existing images, and Dockerfile config. All the sources that you provide are unpacked and merged together in the build directory, which will be processed by the builder image during the build. The option that we will use (and actually have used a few times already) in this book is GitHub repositories.

As we mentioned previously, the precise way in which a build works depends on the build type. You will be able to define the type of build by specifying the build strategy. You can create images using Docker, Source-to-image of custom builds. The build type that is most interesting for us is the source-to-image build, which we will explain in the next section.

There is also another type of build—`pipeline`. The `pipeline` build is connected to the Jenkins CI server and allows you to create a fully featured **Continuous Deployment (CD)** `pipeline`. We will describe this kind of build thoroughly in the second part of this chapter.

Let's turn to the source-to-image build now.

Learning about the source-to-image build

As we mentioned, the source-to-image build needs a builder image and you have to provide it each time when you are configuring such a build. The builder images contain scripts that are responsible for assembling and running the application. The assembling scripts will be run in phase 3 of the build algorithm, and the run script will be used as the start command of the resulting Docker image. During the build, the layer that contains the runnable application will be added on top of the builder image, the run script will be set as the image starting command, and the resulting image will be committed.

We know the basics of source-to-image builds, so now we can explain what we did when deploying our application in the last chapters. Let's start with the following command that we have invoked before running any builds:

```
oc create -f
https://raw.githubusercontent.com/wildfly-swarm/sti-wildflyswarm/master/1.0
/wildflyswarm-sti-all.json
```

The preceding command is responsible for including a YAML object file into our cluster. The main object created by this script is the Docker build configuration. If we examine our cluster using command-line tools, we will find that the new build config is created:

```
[tomek@fedoralaptop ~]$ oc describe bc/wildflyswarm-10-centos7-build
Name:           wildflyswarm-10-centos7-build
Namespace:      petstore
Created:        25 hours ago
Labels:         <none>
Annotations:    <none>
Latest Version: 1

Strategy:       Docker
URL:            git://github.com/wildfly-swarm/sti-wildflyswarm.git
ContextDir:     1.0
From Image:     ImageStreamTag swarm-centos:latest
Output to:      ImageStreamTag wildflyswarm-10-centos7:latest

Build Run Policy:      Serial
Triggered by:          ImageChange
Webhook GitHub:
        URL:    https://192.168.42.201:8443/oapi/v1/namespaces/petstore/buildconfigs/wildflyswarm-10-cen
tos7-build/webhooks/secret101/github

Build                                  Status      Duration    Creation Time
wildflyswarm-10-centos7-build-1        complete    2m40s       2017-10-28 23:37:33 +0200 CEST

Events: <none>
[tomek@fedoralaptop ~]$ 
```

This is the build config for our builder image. We may now examine builds in the Web Console. We will be able to see that the build based on `wildfyswarm-10-centos7` config has already been executed:

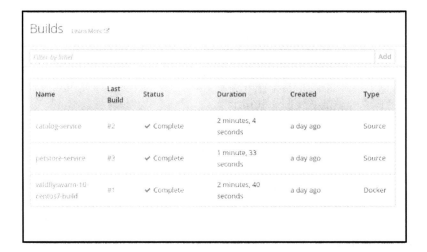

After the execution of the first command, the builder image was created and stored in the cluster. We can confirm this by navigating to **Build | Images** in the web console:

Name	Docker Repo	Tags	Updated
catalog-service	172.30.1.1:5000/petstore/catalog-service	latest	4 hours ago
swarm-centos	172.30.1.1:5000/petstore/swarm-centos	latest	4 hours ago
wildflyswarm-10-centos7	172.30.1.1:5000/petstore/wildflyswarm-10-centos7	latest	4 hours ago

Image Streams   Learn More

Filter by label

As you will have noticed in the preceding screenshot, we have a new image, **wildflyswarm-10-centos7**, available in the cluster. An important thing to note here is that these images have been described as `ImageStreams`. What does that actually mean? `ImageStream`, as its name suggests, is an object that represents a stream of related objects. In our scenario, the `ImageStream` contains all images that are the result of the build of the builder image.

> We created the BuildConfig for the builder image. The source for this image can change; if that happens, OpenShift will create a new version of this image and add it to the `ImageStream`.

The images in the stream can be tagged, and there is always the latest tag, which represents the latest image in the stream.

Let's now examine the `new-app` command that we have used before:

```
oc new-app wildflyswarm-10-
centos7~https://github.com/PacktPublishing/Hands-On-Cloud-Development-with-
WildFly.git (...)
```

We are now ready to explain what the `new-app` syntax means. It has two parts separated by a tilde. The first one is the name of the builder-image stream. The second one is the GitHub repository from which the application will be built.

After we know the internals of the source-to-image build, we can run the build again and examine the build log.

First, we have to remove the `pricing-service` that we have deployed previously:

```
oc delete all -l app=pricing-service
```

After that, we are ready to execute the `new-app` command and use web console to inspect the log:

```
Default locale: en_US, platform encoding: ANSI_X3.4-1968                                    Follow
OS name: "linux", version: "4.4.41-boot2docker", arch: "amd64", family: "unix"
[INFO] Scanning for projects...
Downloading: https://repo.maven.apache.org/maven2/org/jboss/spec/jboss-javaee-7.0/1.0.3.Final/jboss-javaee-7.0-1.0.3.Final.pom
3/17 KB
5/17 KB
8/17 KB
11/17 KB
13/17 KB
16/17 KB
17/17 KB

Downloaded: https://repo.maven.apache.org/maven2/org/jboss/spec/jboss-javaee-7.0/1.0.3.Final/jboss-javaee-7.0-1.0.3.Final.pom (17 KB at
23.4 KB/sec)
Downloading: https://repo.maven.apache.org/maven2/org/jboss/jboss-parent/16/jboss-parent-16.pom
3/31 KB
5/31 KB
8/31 KB
11/31 KB
13/31 KB
16/31 KB
19/31 KB
21/31 KB
24/31 KB
27/31 KB
29/31 KB
```

Oops! We have to download all the dependencies. This fact will result in build taking a substantial amount of time:

```
[INFO] Installing /opt/app-root/src/pom.xml to /opt/app-
root/src/.m2/repository/org/packt/book/pricing-service/1.0/pricing-service-1.0.pom
[INFO] Installing /opt/app-root/src/target/pricing-service-1.0-swarm.jar to /opt/app-
root/src/.m2/repository/org/packt/book/pricing-service/1.0/pricing-service-1.0-swarm.jar
[INFO] ------------------------------------------------------------------------
[INFO] BUILD SUCCESS
[INFO] ------------------------------------------------------------------------
[INFO] Total time: 07:29 min
[INFO] Finished at: 2017-10-30T00:19:09+00:00
[INFO] Final Memory: 31M/234M
[INFO] ------------------------------------------------------------------------
[WARNING] The requested profile "openshift" could not be activated because it does not
exist.
...done

Pushing image 172.30.1.1:5000/petstore/pricing-service:latest ...
Pushed 7/8 layers, 88% complete
Pushed 8/8 layers, 100% complete
Push successful
                                                                         Go to Top
```

This was just a first build. So, what will happen when we run the build for the second time? You can use the web console to force the second build and inspect the log to verify that the dependencies are downloaded again.

This is a serious inconvenience, as it results in much longer build types. Can we do something about it? Yes, we can use incremental builds.

The incremental build is a feature of the source-to-image build, which extracts the build artifacts from the previously created image and uses them to build the next one.

 Our builder image uses the Maven plugin to build a Swarm application, so the artifacts that are being downloaded are the Maven dependency JARs. Usually, different build tools and different types of the artifact will be used. As a result, the specific type of incremental build has to be implemented by the image provider.

In the case of a Swarm builder image, the Maven artifacts are being extracted from the last image and placed in the Maven repo of the new one. As a result, artifacts that are being used many times have to be downloaded only once. Furthermore, in order to decrease the time spent downloading the JARs, you can use a Maven mirror.

OK. However, how can we turn the incremental build on? We have to edit the YAML of our build.

Let's use the web console for that. We have to select the `pricing-service` build and navigate to **Actions** | **Edit YAML** in the top-right corner of the screen. The YAML has to be edited in the following way:

As you will have noticed in the preceding screenshot, we found the `sourceStrategy` section of the build config and added an incremental property with a value set to `true`. Let's run our build again to see what happens.

In our new build log, we can see two optimistic lines:

```
Pulling image "172.30.1.1:5000/petstore/pricing-service:latest" ...
Restoring saved artifacts from prior build...Found pom.xml... attempting to build with 'mvn -U install -Popenshift -DskipTests '
Apache Maven 3.3.3 (7994120775791599e205a5524ec3e0dfe41d4a06; 2015-04-22T11:57:37+00:00)
Maven home: /usr/local/apache-maven-3.3.3
Java version: 1.8.0_151, vendor: Oracle Corporation
Java home: /usr/lib/jvm/java-1.8.0-openjdk-1.8.0.151-1.b12.el7_4.x86_64/jre
Default locale: en_US, platform encoding: ANSI_X3.4-1968
OS name: "linux", version: "4.4.41-boot2docker", arch: "amd64", family: "unix"
```

The first optimistic line is at the beginning where Maven informs us that the artifacts are being restored and the second one is at the end:

```
9   [INFO] BUILD SUCCESS
0   [INFO] ------------------------------------------------------------
1   [INFO] Total time: 16.347 s
2   [INFO] Finished at: 2017-10-30T01:04:03+00:00
3   [INFO] Final Memory: 31M/341M
4   [INFO] ------------------------------------------------------------
```

The build has taken only `16.347` seconds, not much longer than the standalone Maven build.

Configuring environment variables

When we were deploying our services, we provided an environment variables script for catalog and `pricing-services` that needs to interact with our database. Processing this configuration file is also the responsibility of the source-to-image build. If a user wants to provide environment properties to the build, they have to create a `.s2i` directory in the root of the service's GitHub repository and create an environment file that will contain a list of key-value pairs.

For example, let's recall the configuration file for the `pricing-service`:

```
POSTGRESQL_HOST=pricing-service.petstore.svc
POSTGRESQL_USER=pricing
POSTGRESQL_PASSWORD=pricing
POSTGRESQL_SCHEMA=pricingdb
```

Properties set in this file will be available as environment variables during the image build and during its execution.

The whole source-to-image algorithm

After covering the specifics of the source-to-image build operation, let's recap the steps in Swarm's `s2i` build:

1. The container on which the build will take place is created from the builder image.
2. The sources of an application are injected into the container.
3. If incremental builds are enabled, the Maven artifacts will be restored from the previous build image.
4. If provided, environment variables are set.
5. The assembly script, provided by the image creator, is executed.
6. The image is committed with the start command set to the run script provided by the image creator.

A developer who will like to build their applications using the source-to-image build has to provide the name of the builder image and the source code of an application. A developer can enable the incremental build and provide environment variables.

Source-to-image summary

Now that we have covered how the source-to-image build works internally, it's time to look at it from a wider perspective.

The source-to-image build is another tool provided by OpenShift that abstracts away the details of the Kubernetes cluster, providing a simple interface for the developer. The role of the developer is to provide the source code and the name of the image that will be used to build it. It is the responsibility of the image creator to assemble the Docker image that will be deployed on the cluster.

Again, this leads to the separation of concerns—the builder image provider is responsible for assembling source in an optimal way and the details of those optimizations don't have to be known by the developer.

The performance implications of builds resulting from the build architecture are as follows. The libraries that are needed to perform the build and create the runnable container are located in the builder image, which is created once (and later only updated) inside the cluster. The artifacts that are being downloaded during the build can be restored from previous builds if the incremental build is enabled. Owing to that, the dependencies of the application can be downloaded only once and later reused. This leads to a very fast build time. As you may remember, the build of our pricing service took only about 16 seconds, which is only a few seconds more than standalone Maven builds on a modern workstation.

Moreover, the reproducibility, which is one of the constant benefits of using Docker, holds for builder images also. All the builds are performed using exactly the same image. As a result, it is guaranteed that the build result will be the same on all of your environments.

In addition, since builder images are just standard Docker containers and the explicit builder contract allows tool creators to write builder images easily, there is an wide variaty of Docker builder images that you can use. You, as a developer, already have access to a wide variety of builder images dedicated to number of development tools.

In the end, a source-to-image build tool is a tool that represents the core of the OpenShift philosophy. It provides a simple developer interface, which abstracts away the cluster internals, and under the hood it implements the an optimized build process.

The developer view

Till now, we have explained in detail how the source-to-image build builds an image based on your code. The new-app command does not just create the build though. As you remember, after its execution, we were able to test the working application. Clearly, the build and image are not the only product of the command.

Apart from the `BuildConfiguration`, the new-app command creates the `DeploymentConfiguration` (that we described in `Chapter 6`, *Deploying Applications on the Cloud with OpenShift*) and an `ImageStream` for our application.

Let's take a look at the created objects in the following diagram:

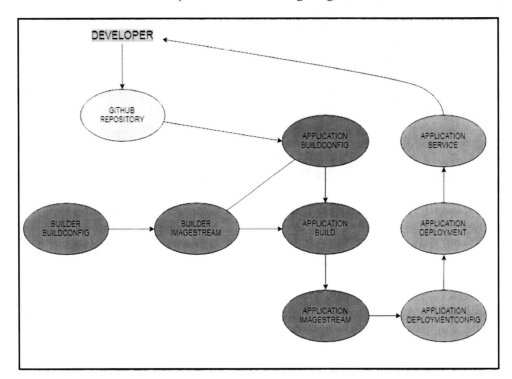

In the preceding diagram, the objects related to the builder image are colored red, build-related objects are colored blue, and deployment-related objects are colored green. The build is triggered by a developer by pushing changes to GitHub. It results in the creation of the build objects. If the build is successful, the image is pushed to the image stream. This further triggers the deployment of the application, which, if successful, results in the creation of application services.

The important thing to note is that, in the simplest scenario, a developer may be responsible only for pushing the changes to the repository—in other words, programming and their changes will be propagated to the cluster.

That's nice again, but, in some scenarios, we will like to have more than that: a full CD `pipeline` with integration tests, checking the deployed application, or staging the changes in different environments. As we hinted earlier, we can integrate an OpenShift cluster with Jenkins to use its full power to implement the CD `pipeline` for our services. Let's learn how to do it.

Pipeline build

In the first chapter, when we were explaining why you may be considering implementing the microservice architecture in your applications, we mentioned the challenges that are being currently faced by application developers and architects.

One of the key tools that may enable us to deal with providing software in a way that enables us to meet those challenges is automation. As we covered in the preceding chapter, OpenShift enables us to automate infrastructure provisioning. However, we need more than that.

We will also like to automate the process of deploying software into production. Ideally, we will like to have tools that will enable us to release software immediately. OpenShift provides such a tool in the form of the build `pipeline`. Let's introduce the rationale behind this concept.

Let's start with CI.

Continuous integration

As a developer, you know too well what the development of projects looks like. There are many developers working on different functionalities, which they contribute to the same repository. Contributions from all the developers have to be integrated into the code repository so that stable code is created. After that, the code can be published into the production environment.

This sounds simple, but if you don't create an organized order according to which this process is executed, you will quickly end up with a huge mess. If the developers will integrate rarely, they are asking for problems. Their repositories will be highly diverged, and the application's functionality will be scattered between their repositories. As a result, during the development, there will be no *current state* source repository, and we will have no information about the state of an application. The new version of an application will emerge during the time people decide to push their contribution to the main code (which will presumably happen the day before the release). The process of integration at this point will be painful, where incompatible contributions are being discovered, and errors will emerge. Such a situation was described in the past as *integration hell*.

Owing to the preceding problems, it became clear that it will be a good idea to integrate code frequently. The methodology that advocates such a behavior and, more importantly, gives hints on how to do it, is called CI.

Obviously, pushing the code frequently to the repository is not helping us much. At each commit, we need to make sure that the current version of the code at least compiles, and passes unit and integration tests. This is by no means a comprehensive list: to declare your code correctly, you may also need automatic code inspections or code reviews to name a few.

In order for this process to be executed consistently, it has to be automated and executed each time the user wants to make the change to the code. Also, developers are supposed to integrate their code frequently, with each logical functionality developed, and are supposed to fix any errors that appear as soon as possible.

If this procedure is observed, this will lead to a number of benefits:

- Problems are detected quickly. As the result, their source can be debugged and fixed quickly.
- The current version of the application is always present—it is the result of the last successful build. At each point, we can tell the status of the application, how it works, and what functionalities have been currently implemented.
- The automated process works as a trigger for quality control. The build is guaranteed to be run and be reproducible.

Continuous deployment

Continuous Integration ensures continuous builds of source code. It demands that fixes are pushed often and provides instant feedback to the developers. What if we extend this notion and configure our build infrastructure so that it will ensure that our services will be built and deployed automatically?

Such an approach, which is an extension of CI, is called Continuous Deployment. To implement it, we will need to automate the release process also. This means that we will have to keep all the resources that are needed to release the software to the given environment, such as environment properties or configuration scripts.

As a reward, we will be able to obtain reliable and repeatable releases. First of all, as the release process is no longer manual, all the magic is taken away from the release process. The release is executed by the release script using environment properties, which are both parts of the versioned build configuration. Those files are the one source-of-truth regarding the build process. As a result, if an error occurs during the build, those scripts have to be fixed. There is no place for manual patches or ad hoc fixes. Also, builds happen often, so configuration bugs will have an opportunity to occur and be fixed. On the other hand, after builds and releases start to work correctly, each next correct build adds more confidence in the release process. As a result, the release becomes a well-tested and an automated event.

 Such an approach changes the way the team works by changing the speed at which features are developed. With CD, you are not releasing the software in large chunks to the client. Instead, small functionalities are released often and are immediately visible to the client.

This is the expected behavior for a number of reasons. First, customers will like to respond to client demand as quickly as possible. Having the tool that enables them to do that will be a big market advantage for the customer. However, there is more to it: because new functionalities are released often, they are visible to the customer immediately. As a result, a customer can immediately assess the actually implemented functionality. This creates an efficient feedback loop between the developers and the customers, which allow for faster convergence to the functionality actually expected by the client.

Deployment pipeline

The process of automatic delivery is implemented using a `pipeline`. A `pipeline` is a chain of steps that takes the source code as its input and provides a working application on it's output.

The goal of the `pipeline` is to make sure that the source code is ready to be deployed in production. As a result, a `pipeline` should be able to catch errors as soon as possible and provide feedback to the developers immediately.

Also, because the final product is the released application, a `pipeline` should automate the release process so that it is run the same in all environments.

Although a `pipeline` is a configurable script and its direct operation depends on your concrete environment, there are a number of common steps that are executed in the deployment `pipeline`: commit, build, automatic tests, manual tests, release, and so on.

Configuring Continuous Deployment in OpenShift environments

After this quick theory recap, now let's return to our cluster and configure CD for our application.

At the beginning of this chapter, we described the source-to-image build, which we have used in previous chapters. We also hinted that there is a `pipeline` build available. As you probably have guessed by now, this is the kind of build that we will use to implement CD of our services.

The `pipeline` build uses the Jenkins server to configure the `pipeline` configuration. Before moving further, let's introduce it quickly.

Introducing Jenkins

Jenkins is an open source software automation server. It allows for `pipeline` creation and provides the relevant syntax. So, how are we able to use Jenkins in OpenShift cluster and configure `pipeline` execution? Let's find out.

Our first pipeline

Let's start by creating our first `pipeline`. We have to log in to our web console and navigate to **Add to project** | **Import YAML**.

In order to do that, we have to go the web console's main web page and navigate to **Add to Project** | **Import YAML/Json** and enter the following script there:

```
apiVersion: v1
kind: BuildConfig
metadata:
  name: pricing-service-pipeline
  labels:
    name: pricing-service-pipeline
spec:
  runPolicy: Serial
  strategy:
    type: JenkinsPipeline
    jenkinsPipelineStrategy:
      jenkinsfile:"pipeline { \n agent any\n stages {\n stage('Build') {\n
steps {\n echo 'Pipeline is running'\n }\n }\n }\n }\n"
```

After the script is created, we can click on the **Create** button:

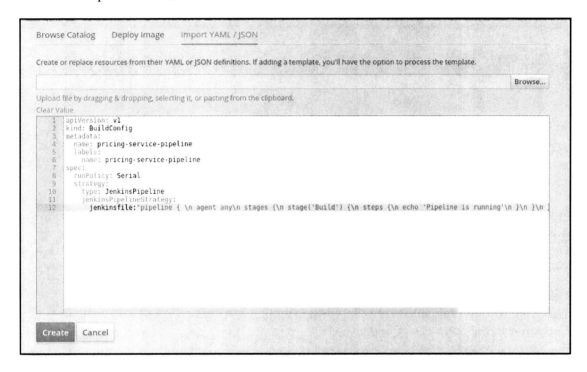

Before we look further at the `pipeline` code, let's note the other things that are happening. If we get to the main view of the web console, we will note that there is a new resource:

Let's take a look at the currently available **Pods** too:

Indeed, there is a new deployment of Jenkins server running, and the container for the Jenkins server is being created. OpenShift runs a `pipeline` build using the Jenkins server. Therefore, whenever you create a `pipeline`, OpenShift must check whether there is a Jenkins server present in the cluster. If not, OpenShift will start one automatically.

The creation of the Jenkins server takes some time, so we have to wait till it has been deployed. After we are able to see that the application is running in the **Pods** view, we are ready to start the build of our first `pipeline`.

In order to do that, let's navigate to **Build | Pipelines**. You will be able to see that there is a new `pipeline` present:

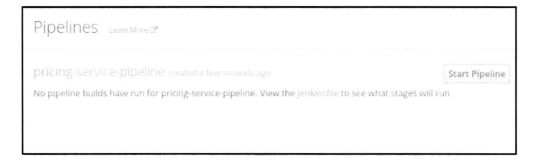

Let's click on the **Start Pipeline** button and see what happens:

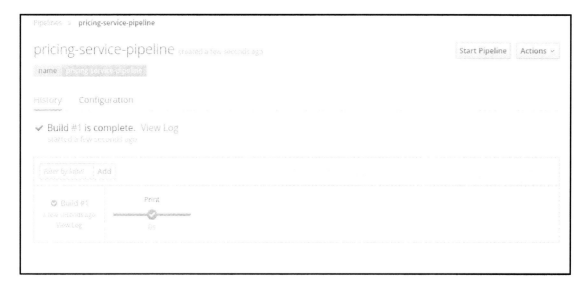

Note in the preceding screenshot that the build has run. The dot with the tick described as Print means that one stage has been run and that it has been successful. We will be talking about the Jenkins `pipeline` structure in just a moment. Now, let's take a look at more information about our current build by clicking on the **View Log** button:

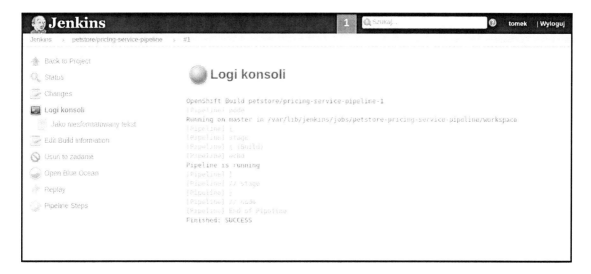

As you will have noticed in the preceding screenshot, we have been redirected to the Jenkins console. The build has been created, the **Print** stage has been executed, and the print message that we have echoed has indeed been written to a log.

As you can see, the `pipeline` build configuration has been automatically turned into the Jenkins build and run in the Jenkins console. We will get more information about the build when we click on **petstore/pricing-service-pipeline** in the top-left corner of the screen:

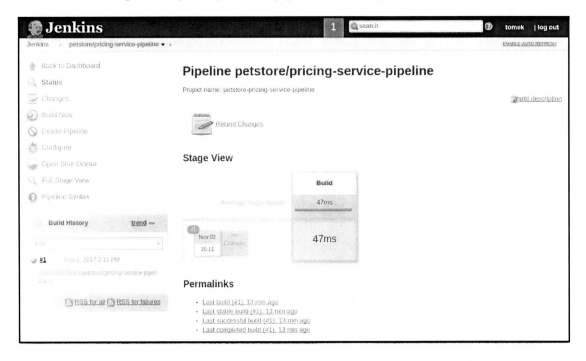

From this window, we can trace the build history, view the logs and time of the latest execution, or edit the `pipeline`, among others. At this point, it is good to look again at the script that we have written in order to create the `pipeline`. You probably have noted immediately that the Jenkins `pipeline` was squashed into one line, making it hard to read and edit. Before we take any other steps, let's find a human way to edit our `pipeline`.

In order to do that, let's click on the **Configure** button on the left-hand side menu and scroll down:

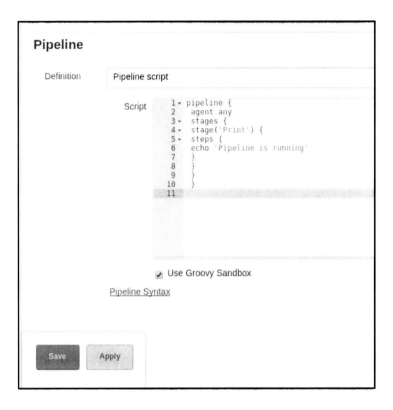

We have a good editor for our `pipeline` here. Let's make our first edit of the file:

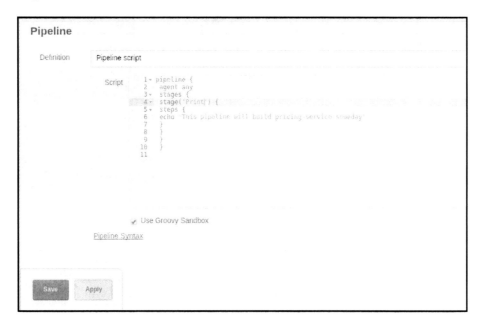

We will then test it to check whether it works. In order to do that, we have to save the `pipeline` and click on the **Build Now** button in the build view. After that, we are ready to examine the log by clicking on the second build that has just been executed:

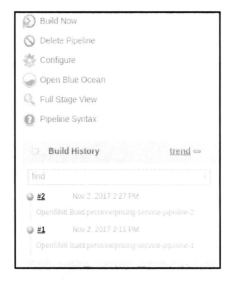

We will see the new log as follows:

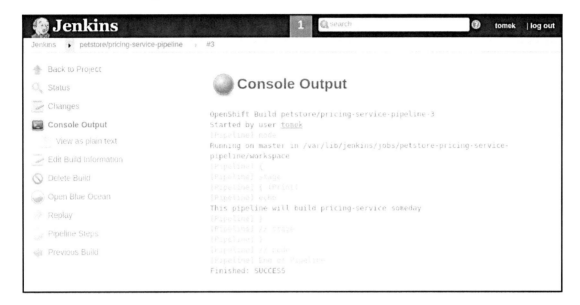

Also, let's log in again to the web console and examine that `pipeline` there:

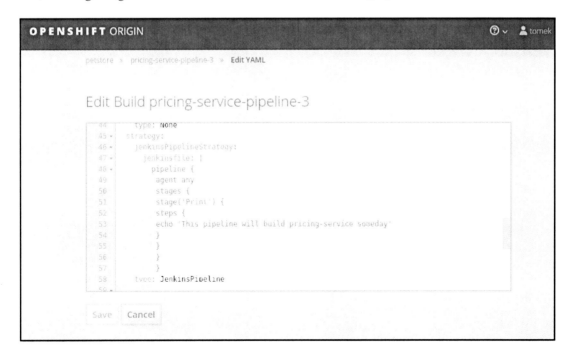

As you will have noticed, the `pipeline` build config was modified accordingly to the changes that we have made in Jenkins. We will perform our future changes using the Jenkins server.

The new message that we are printing in the build promises that our build will do something useful at some point. After all, we want to create a CD `pipeline` for our services and not print messages. Before we can do it though, we will need to learn a few more things. In the beginning, we will need to say a few more words about the language that we are using to define the `pipeline`.

Pipeline syntax language

When we wrote our first `pipeline`, we used the Jenkins declarative pipeline language. We will describe the essentials of the **Declarative Pipeline Language (DPL)** in the next section.

Core pipeline elements

In order to do that, let's return to the `pipeline` that we executed in the preceding section:

```
//1
pipeline {
    //2
    agent any
    //3
    stages {
        //4
        stage('Print') {
            steps {
                echo 'This pipeline will build pricing-service one day'
            }
        }
    }
}
```

Each `pipeline` in DPL must be enclosed with the `pipeline` block (1).

The `pipeline` must begin with the `agent` directive (2). This directive specifies the Jenkins builder machines in which the build stages (more about them in a moment) can be executed. This setting can be overridden in each of the stages. In our examples, we will use any agent for all the stages.

The core `pipeline` build blocks are the stages. The stages are meant to map to the stages in the CD `pipeline`. They are defined in a serial order, and each stage can execute only if the stage before has succeeded.

The stages have to be enclosed with the `stages` (3) block. Each stage (there need to be at least one of them) has its own `stage` block with the name specified as a parameter.

Each stage block can contain a bunch of directives followed by the steps block, which encloses one or more steps that will be executed in the `pipeline`.

Now, we are getting to the key point. What are the available steps that we can execute? Jenkins provides a very large number of different steps provided by different plugins. We will concentrate on one specific plugin that makes it easy to develop and execute operations on OpenShift clusters—let's discuss OpenShift, the `pipeline` Jenkins plugin (Further reading, link 1).

Standard Maven operation

The first stage that we will implement is the unit testing stage. In the beginning, we will add a simple unit test in the same way that we did in `Chapter 5`, *Testing Your Services with Arquillian*. We have to extend `pom.xml`:

```
(...)

    <dependencies>
        (...)
        <dependency>
            <groupId>org.postgresql</groupId>
            <artifactId>postgresql</artifactId>
            <version>${version.postgresql}</version>
        </dependency>

        //1
        <dependency>
            <groupId>junit</groupId>
            <artifactId>junit</artifactId>
            <version>${version.junit}</version>
            <scope>test</scope>
        </dependency>

        //2
        <dependency>
            <groupId>org.jboss.arquillian.junit</groupId>
```

```
                <artifactId>arquillian-junit-container</artifactId>
                <scope>test</scope>
        </dependency>

        //3
        <dependency>
                <groupId>org.wildfly.swarm</groupId>
                <artifactId>arquillian</artifactId>
                <version>${version.wildfly.swarm}</version>
                <scope>test</scope>
        </dependency>

        //4
        <dependency>
                <groupId>com.h2database</groupId>
                <artifactId>h2</artifactId>
                <version>${version.h2}</version>
                <scope>test</scope>
        </dependency>

    </dependencies>

    (...)




</project>
```

Recall that we had to add dependencies for JUnit (1), Arquillian (2), Swarm's Arquillian adapter (3), and the in-memory database that we will use (4).

Secondly, we have to provide test resources, namely `persistence.xml`:

```
<?xml version="1.0" encoding="UTF-8"?>
<persistence
        xmlns:xsi="http://www.w3.org/2001/XMLSchema-instance"
        version="2.1"
        xmlns="http://xmlns.jcp.org/xml/ns/persistence"
        xsi:schemaLocation="http://xmlns.jcp.org/xml/ns/persistence
http://xmlns.jcp.org/xml/ns/persistence/persistence_2_1.xsd">
    <!-- 1 -->
    <persistence-unit name="PricingPU" transaction-type="JTA">
        <!-- 2 -->
        <jta-data-source>java:jboss/datasources/PricingDS</jta-data-source>
        <properties>
            <!-- 3 -->
            <property name="javax.persistence.schema-
```

```
generation.database.action" value="drop-and-create"/>
            <property name="javax.persistence.schema-generation.create-
source" value="metadata"/>
            <property name="javax.persistence.schema-generation.drop-
source" value="metadata"/>

            <property name="javax.persistence.sql-load-script-source"
value="META-INF/load.sql"/>
        </properties>
    </persistence-unit>
</persistence>
```

And the load script that we are going to use to test the database:

```
DROP TABLE IF EXISTS PRICE;

CREATE TABLE PRICE (id serial PRIMARY KEY, name varchar, price smallint);

INSERT INTO PRICE(name, price) VALUES ('test-pet', 5);
```

Ensure that we also add the h2 driver module:

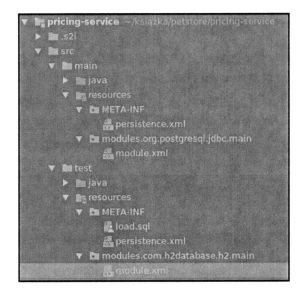

We are now ready to write a test:

```
package org.packt.swarm.petstore.pricing;

import org.jboss.arquillian.container.test.api.Deployment;
import org.jboss.arquillian.junit.Arquillian;
import org.jboss.shrinkwrap.api.ShrinkWrap;
import org.jboss.shrinkwrap.api.asset.EmptyAsset;
import org.jboss.shrinkwrap.api.spec.JavaArchive;
import org.junit.Assert;
import org.junit.Test;
import org.junit.runner.RunWith;
import org.wildfly.swarm.Swarm;
import org.wildfly.swarm.arquillian.CreateSwarm;
import org.wildfly.swarm.datasources.DatasourcesFraction;
import org.wildfly.swarm.jaxrs.JAXRSArchive;
import org.wildfly.swarm.spi.api.Module;

import javax.inject.Inject;

//1
@RunWith(Arquillian.class)
public class PricingServiceTest {

    //2
    @Deployment
    public static JavaArchive createDeployment() {
        return ShrinkWrap.create(JavaArchive.class)
                .addClasses(Price.class, PricingService.class)
                .addAsResource("META-INF/persistence.xml")
                .addAsResource("META-INF/load.sql")
                .addAsManifestResource(EmptyAsset.INSTANCE, "beans.xml");
    }

    //2
    @CreateSwarm
    public static Swarm createSwarm() throws Exception {
        DatasourcesFraction datasourcesFraction = new DatasourcesFraction()
                //3
                .jdbcDriver("h2", (d) -> {
                    d.driverClassName("org.h2.Driver");
                    d.xaDatasourceClass("org.h2.jdbcx.JdbcDataSource");
                    d.driverModuleName("com.h2database.h2");
                })
                .dataSource("PricingDS", (ds) -> {
                    ds.driverName("h2");
ds.connectionUrl("jdbc:h2:mem:test;DB_CLOSE_DELAY=-1;DB_CLOSE_ON_EXIT=FALSE
");
```

```
            ds.userName("sa");
            ds.password("sa");
        });

    Swarm swarm = new Swarm();
    swarm.fraction(datasourcesFraction);

    return swarm;
}

//3
@Inject
PricingService pricingService;

//4
@Test
public void testSearchById() {
    Assert.assertEquals(pricingService.findByName("test-
pet").getPrice(),5);
    }
}
```

Now, we are finally ready to write the testing stage. We will like to make this stage run fast and fail immediately if there are some problems, without creating an image or changing anything in our OpenShift model. For this, we will use standard Maven and git from the command line.

In order to do this, we need to configure those tools. To do this, we will have to go to Jenkins configuration in the main menu, click on **Manage Jenkins** and select the tool configuration for **JDK**:

And **Maven**:

We are finally ready to update our `pipeline`. Let's take a look:

```
pipeline {
//1
 agent any
//2
tools {
    maven 'maven3.5.2'
    jdk 'jdk8u152'
    git 'Default'
 }
 stages {
//3
 stage('Unit tests') {
     steps {
       //4
       git url:
'https://github.com/PacktPublishing/Hands-On-Cloud-Development-with-WildFly
.git'
 //5
 sh 'mvn clean test -Dswarm.build.modules=target/test-classes/modules'
 }
 }
}
```

We have provided the mandatory agent any (1) and configured Maven, JDK, and git tools, providing the versions for all of them. We have replaced our print stage with the unit test stage (3), which consists of the following two steps:

1. The first step clones the **pricing-service**'s git repository (4)
2. The second step runs the Maven tests (5)

We have to provide the modules directory in order for the tests to work.

OK. So, we have our first stage. Now, what next? If the unit tests pass, we will like to build and deploy an image with our application. In order to do that, we will have to interact with our cluster object from within the `pipeline`. The tool that will help us do that with ease is the OpenShift Pipeline Plugin. Let's learn more about it.

OpenShift Pipeline Plugin

Jenkins has a pluggable architecture, which allows for plugin development. OpenShift provides its own plugin, which allows for straightforward operations on OpenShift cluster objects in a declarative manner. The plugin provides a number of commands. We will introduce them one by one during the `pipeline` development.

In the beginning, we will write a build stage, which will assemble the image and ensure that the application works correctly.

The first command that we will use is the `openShiftBuild` command. It allows running one of the builds defined in the OpenShift cluster. This command takes one mandatory parameter, `buildCfg`, which is the name of the build that will be executed.

The second command that we will use is verified as `Build`. This command also takes `buildCfg` and checks whether the last build of this type has finished successfully within a reasonable time period. To set the period, we will use the `waitTime` parameter.

Let's take a look at our new `pipeline`:

```
pipeline {
 agent any
 tools {
    maven 'maven3.5.2'
    jdk 'jdk8u152'
    git 'Default'
 }
 stages {
 stage('Test') {
     steps {
       git url:
'https://github.com/PacktPublishing/Hands-On-Cloud-Development-with-WildFly
.git'
       sh 'mvn clean install -Dswarm.build.modules=target/test-
classes/modules'
     }
   }
 //1
 stage('Build') {
     steps {
        //2
        openshiftBuild(bldCfg: 'pricing-service', showBuildLogs: 'true')
        //3
        openshiftVerifyBuild(bldCfg: 'pricing-service', waitTime: '300000')
     }
   }
   }
 }
```

We have introduced the `Build` stage (1) and added two steps to it, as mentioned in the preceding paragraph. The `Build` command runs the `pricing-service s2i` build that we configured at the beginning of this chapter (2). The verify command checks whether the build was executed successfully within 5 minutes.

 We will like to only build the image here and not deploy it yet. So, we will need to modify our build and remove the image change as the trigger for the deployment.

After that, we are ready to start our Build in Jenkins. If you do it and click on console output, you will be able to see the execution log. Let's take a look at it:

```
            at org.apache.maven.surefire.booter.ProviderFactory.invokeProvider(ProviderFactory.java:85)
            at org.apache.maven.surefire.booter.ForkedBooter.runSuitesInProcess(ForkedBooter.java:115)
            at org.apache.maven.surefire.booter.ForkedBooter.main(ForkedBooter.java:75)


 Results :

 Failed tests:   testSearchById(org.packt.swarm.petstore.pricing.PricingServiceTest)

 Tests run: 1, Failures: 1, Errors: 0, Skipped: 0

 [INFO] ------------------------------------------------------------------------
 [INFO] BUILD FAILURE
```

Oops! If you look again at the test, you will note that there is an error, as the price of the test-pet is 5 none 7. Before we fix it, let's note how the pipeline works. Our first unit test stage failed immediately. As a result, no further stages were started. No images were built and no applications were deployed. Let's also look at the pipeline view on the web console:

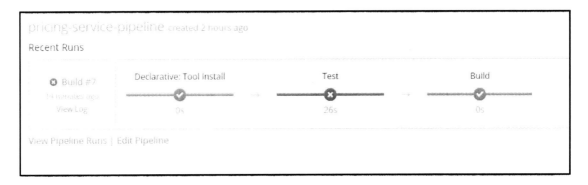

The console presents the `pipeline` execution in a graphic way, showing that the test stage failed. Let's fix our tests and run the application again. If you do it and look at the console log, you will be able to see that the test has passed and the `Build` stage has been executed:

```
[WARNING] The requested profile "openshift" could not be activated because it does not exist.
...done
Pushing image 172.30.1.1:5000/petstore/pricing-service:latest ...
Pushed 7/8 layers, 88% complete
Pushed 7/8 layers, 95% complete
Pushed 8/8 layers, 100% complete
Push successful

Exiting "Trigger OpenShift Build" successfully; build "pricing-service-19" has completed with status:  [Complete].
[Pipeline] openshiftVerifyBuild


Starting the "Verify OpenShift Build" step with build config "pricing-service" from the project "petstore".
  Waiting on build "pricing-service-19" to complete ...
Operation will timeout after 5000 milliseconds


Exiting "Verify OpenShift Build" successfully; build "pricing-service-19" has completed with status:  [Complete].
[Pipeline] }
[Pipeline] // stage
[Pipeline] }
[Pipeline] // withEnv
[Pipeline] }
[Pipeline] // node
[Pipeline] End of Pipeline
Finished: SUCCESS
```

When you take a look at the web console, you will be able to see that the `Build` has been finished and that the image has been created:

Let's look at the currently available deployments:

Now, we only have the build image and have not triggered the deployment yet. Let's add another stage to our build. We will use openshiftDeploy, openshiftScale, openShiftVerifyDeployment, and openShiftVerifyService. Before doing that, let's introduce each of these commands.

The openshiftDeploy command takes a mandatory parameter—dplCfg—which is the name of the deployment. It runs the deployment of an application.

openshiftScale, irrespective of a mandatory dplCfg parameter, takes the replicaCount parameter, which specifies the number of replicas of the application. Since we are using this command to scale the application, we will change the number of instance deployments in the deploymentConfig to zero. As a result, the pods will be started only after the openshiftScale operation has been executed without an unnecessary rescale.

openShiftVerifyDeployment has the same mandatory parameter as the two previous commands—dplCfg. This command has three optional parameters, and we will use all of them:

- replicaCount: This parameter specifies the expected number of replicas
- verifyReplicaCount: This is a Boolean parameter, which specifies whether the replica count should be checked
- waitTime: This indicates the time in milliseconds in which we should wait for the verification
- openshiftVerifyService: This command checks whether the service is available

`openshiftVerifyService` has one mandatory parameter:

- `svcName`
- One optional parameter `retryCount` specifies how many times the connection is attempted before declaring the verification invalid

Before showing you the new script, we will introduce one more concept. As we mentioned in the theoretical section of this chapter, the build should give immediate feedback to its authors regarding its status. In order to react to the `Build` status, the DPL provides the ability to perform an action after the `pipeline` is finished based on the status of the build. The construct that allows doing that is post directive.

A post directive enables us to perform an action after the build has been finished. It can be placed at the end of the `pipeline` or at the end of each stage. The post directive provides a bunch of subdirectories: always, success, failure, unstable, (runs if the build is unstable—the result changes during the build) aborted, and changed.

In our script, for the sake of simplicity, we will echo the build status to the console, but we can use the available Jenkins plugins0; to configure email, HipChat, or slack notification.

Let's take a look at the build:

```
pipeline {
 agent any
 tools {
    maven 'maven3.5.2'
    jdk 'jdk8u152'
    git 'Default'
 }
 stages {
 stage('Test') {
     steps {
      git url:
'https://github.com/PacktPublishing/Hands-On-Cloud-Development-with-WildFly
.git'
      sh 'mvn clean install -Dswarm.build.modules=target/test-
classes/modules'
     }
    }
  stage('Build') {
     steps {
        openshiftBuild(bldCfg: 'pricing-service', showBuildLogs: 'true')
        openshiftVerifyBuild(bldCfg: 'pricing-service', waitTime: '300000')
     }
    }
```

```
//1
  stage('Deploy'){
      steps {
          //2
          openshiftDeploy(depCfg: 'pricing-service')
          //3
          openshiftScale(depCfg: 'pricing-service',replicaCount:'3')
          //4
          openshiftVerifyDeployment(depCfg: 'pricing-
service',verifyReplicaCount:'true',replicaCount:'3', waitTime: '300000')
          //5
          openshiftVerifyService(svcName: 'pricing-service')
      }
  }
  }
  post {
      //6
      success {
          echo "Job '${env.JOB_NAME} [${env.BUILD_NUMBER}]' result: SUCCESS"
      }
      //7
      failure {
          echo "Job '${env.JOB_NAME} [${env.BUILD_NUMBER}]' result: FAILURE"
      }
  }
  }
```

We have extended our `pipeline` in a way described previously:

1. We have added the `Deploy` stage (1), which deploys the application (2)
2. Then, it scales the application (3)
3. It verifies that the deployment succeeded (4) and that the service is available (5)
4. After each build, the result of the test is echoed to the output, depending on whether the test succeeded (6) or failed (7)

If you look at the console output, you will be able to see that all the steps that we have implemented have been executed successfully.

You can also verify this in the web console `pipeline` view:

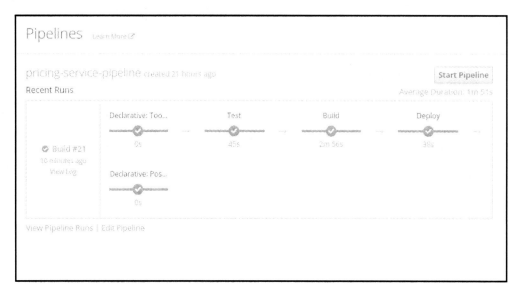

Finally, you can verify in the web console that the service has indeed been created and that the corresponding pods are running.

Summary

In this chapter, you learned the build infrastructure provided by OpenShift. You then learned to use source-to-image build, which abstracts away the details of Kubernetes internals from the developer and lets them build the image based solely on code with minimal configuration.

In the second part of this chapter, you learned about the `pipeline` build, which, effectively, is a way to integrate Jenkins `pipelines` with OpenShift infrastructures. You also learned how to create the `pipeline` build and the basics of the DPL syntax. Hence, you were able to create a CD `pipeline` for your petstore's `pricing-service`.

Further reading

https://jenkins.io/doc/book/pipeline/syntax/

10
Providing Security Using Keycloak

In this chapter, we will learn the basics of distributed, token-based security. We will introduce Keycloak—an authentication server that can be used to secure distributed cloud applications. As a practical example, we will secure part of the API of the Petstore application.

Token-based security

Keycloak uses token-based security protocols. In order to understand how they work, we will introduce basic information about them.

Rationale

In applications that are built using the client-server architecture, the server is often responsible for implementing security. A client provides credentials to the server, which is responsible for authenticating and authorizing users.

This model doesn't work well with distributed applications that require over-the-network invocations between a number of independent services.

First of all, an architecture in which each service is responsible for implementing security is unscalable. We would preferably like to create a server that is responsible for keeping the data about users and implementing authentication and authorization. All other services will need to rely on it whenever any security decision has to be made.

here is a diagram of how this may look:

This solution has a fundamental flaw: credential sharing.

> In a cloud environment, an invocation may span a number of
> heterogeneous services, and, in general, we can't assume that those
> services can be trusted. If at least one of the clients with whom the user
> has shared its credentials is compromised, then all the systems are
> compromised.

However, there is another, more subtle problem. In the preceding architecture, it is unable
to distinguish between invocation by the user and invocation on behalf of the user. For
example, let's suppose that **SERVICE B** is a disk storage service and **SERVICE A** needs to
obtain a file from it on behalf of the user. If the user propagates their credentials to A, then
A can do whatever the user can do (for example, delete all their files). This is clearly
undesirable.

The preceding problems led to the emergence of the protocols based on security tokens.

Let's look at those in greater detail now.

A basic architecture

Let's start by introducing the essential concept of access tokens as follows:

An access token is a string representing a set of authorization credentials issued to the client. When a client wants to perform a request on behalf of a user, it needs to obtain their permission to do so. The token represents such a permission.

An access token is created for a specific client. As a result, a user can limit the permissions associated with an access token and therefore the client.

An access token contains authorization information—based on the access token, a service can decide whether the client who performs the invocation is allowed to perform the given operation. An access token does not contain information about the user, and possession of the access token does not imply that the request is being performed by a user.

For example, a typical flow of the distributed protocol that uses an access token is as follows:

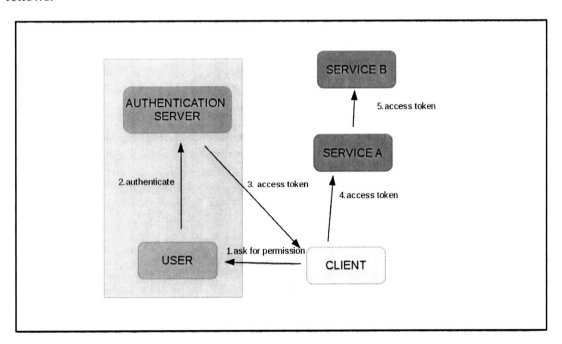

Note the following things in the preceding example:

1. The client wants to perform the request on **SERVICE A**, but needs user permission to do that. Because of this, it asks the user for that permission.
2. If the user agrees, she authenticates to the authentication server (2).
3. If the authentication finishes with success, the server generates an **access token**, which is sent to the client (3).
4. The client can use this token to access **SERVICE A** on behalf of the user (4).
5. Furthermore, the token can be propagated to other services (5).

Let's emphasize the most important characteristics of such an architecture:

The authorization (no matter which method it uses) happens solely between the user and the authentication server. No other component gains access to any kind of user credentials. As a result, the authorization server is the only component that has to be fully trusted.

Access tokens represent permission to do something on behalf of a user and are generated for the individual client. Because of that, an **access token** issued to a given client can contain a minimal set of permissions that will allow it to do its job. Furthermore, if the token is propagated to a compromised client or is stolen, it can do much less harm than just leaking of user credentials. Nevertheless, to minimize the impact of such a situation, access tokens are issued for a short period of time. As a result, even if a token is stolen, there is only a small time frame in which it can be used (concrete protocols may define a way for the client to refresh an access token).

To sum up, token-based security protocols allow the implementation of decentralized authentication and authorization: users authenticate to a trusted authentication server and obtain tokens that can be used to authorize access to services. This is especially useful in cloud architecture: based on tokens generated by a trusted authentication server, we can gain access to a number of heterogeneous services distributed across the network, providing them with the ability to perform operations on our behalf, ensuring that the set of permissions associated with the token is minimal for the services to do their job.

There are a number of protocols that standardize this type of distributed security. One of them is **OpenID Connect (OIDC)**, which is the modern protocol used by Keycloak by default; we will use it in our examples. Let's look at it a bit more closely.

OpenID Connect

OIDC is built on top of the **Oauth2** protocol, which is an open standard for delegating access. Oauth2 specifies directly how this process, outlined in the preceding paragraph should be executed, which actors will take part in it, and how and in which order they should cooperate to obtain the access token and use it for authorization. The hitch is that Oauth2 specifies only that, leaving a very wide margin to its implementations. As a result, it can be thought of as a framework used to build protocols rather than as a protocol itself.

OIDC is a protocol that was created using this framework. It fills the implementation gaps (such as the token format) and adds authentication information, which Oauth2 lacks. OIDC standardizes the way in which information about the user can be obtained.

The gritty details of the protocols are beyond the scope of this book. If you are interested in those, refer to the protocol specifications (Further reading, link 1,2). In this chapter, we will teach you the minimum needed for you to understand Keycloak configuration for the basic usage of distributed security, which we will be presenting in the following example.

OIDC specifies the number of flows—procedures that describe the process of obtaining and using tokens in detail. In the following section, we will take a look at the authentication code flow, the default flow used by Keycloak.

Authentication code flow

In this section, we will describe authentication code flow. This is a precise description, which, as you will see, will directly impact on the configuration of the authentication server. It assumes that client is a web application running inside the browser. As a result, you should interpret the terms used literally. For example, if we talk about a client redirecting a user to an authentication server, we literally mean the HTTP redirect of a browser to an address of an authentication server. As we've already suggested, you will see those operations later in this chapter, when we will finish securing the pet store application.

Let's take a look at a diagram of the flow now:

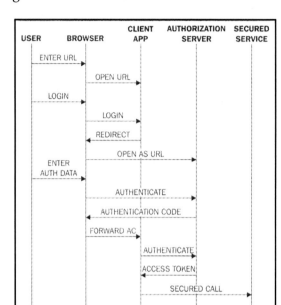

The user uses the client, which is a browser-based application. When, at some point, a user performs a login operation, they are automatically redirected to the authentication server. Authentication is performed between the authentication server and user. The client has nothing to do with it: the way in which it was performed is too opaque for it, and the client has no interaction with any credentials provided by the user, no matter what kind of authentication method is used. As a result, the credentials are provided only to one entity on the web; if it is not compromised, then they will not be compromised either.

If the authentication process finishes with success, the authentication server will generate an authentication code: a very short-lived, single-use code that will redirect the user to the client. The client will authenticate itself to an authentication server using the code and its own credentials. If the client authenticates correctly, an authentication server will generate an access token and return it to a client. Why is this step necessary? As we've already mentioned in the preceding section, an access token has to be generated for the resource owner, that is, the client tuple. Both the user and the client have to authenticate themselves to the authentication server in order to generate the token. The authentication server knows which permissions should be delegated to the client and creates an authentication token accordingly.

Apart from an access token, the user obtains an ID token and, optionally, a refresh token.

We have mentioned that OIDC also provides information on the authentication. This is true. This information is provided to the client in the ID token. An ID token, in contrast with the access token, which may be opaque to the client, contains information provided for the client, and cannot be used to gain access to resources. To put it in a different way, an ID token is a token that is generated for the client and allows them to read information about the user. We will use this capability in our example.

We have also mentioned that a protocol may specify the way to refresh an access token. OIDC does that by using a refresh token. A refresh token allows a client to create a new **access token**, which, as we've mentioned, is short-lived when the old one expires. A client can use a refresh token in order to keep their authorization valid for a required period without having to delegate a new access code (making the user authenticate again). A client should keep a refresh token confidential—even if the access token is compromised, it can be used only for a short period, and only a client would be able to obtain a new one.

As you will see in *WildFly Swarm Keycloak adapter* section, we will be dealing directly with access tokens (we have to propagate them between our services), but not with other tokens, as their functionality is encapsulated behind APIs. Let's continue with the flow.

After the client obtains the access token, it sends it to the resource server with the request. The resource server has to verify that the token is correct, extract the authorization data in it, and decide whether the request should be allowed.

Access tokens that we will use in the example application are bearer tokens. This means that any entity that possesses these token can use them in the same way. As a result, the tokens can be propagated to all of the microservices in our application (which we will take advantage of soon). On the flip side, this means that the leak of the token is dangerous and, as a result, a bearer token cannot be sent by an untrusted network (we will get to that at the end of this chapter).

We have now introduced enough theory already and, as usual, after a harsh technical introduction, we will head over to the practical section: a land of milk and honey, where the tools do everything for us. Let's jump into that right away!

Introducing Keycloak

In order to secure our Petstore application, we will use Keycloak. Keycloak is an open source, **single sign-on** (SSO) identity management server, which supports, among others, OIDC-based security.

Keycloak is equipped with a convenient, web-based UI, which enables us to configure all aspect of its behavior using the graphical interface. Furthermore, services that we will write have to be integrated with Keycloak as well. In order to make this integration easy, Keycloak provides a bunch of adapters, which are components that can be installed into any given type of service. In the following example, we will discuss how to use both of those tools.

Before we start, let's outline the functionality that we will be adding to the pet store application.

Cart-service

Until this point, all the services that we've implemented could be accessed by anonymous users. In this chapter, we will implement the cart functionality. Obviously, in order to add something to the cart, you have to be authenticated in the application:

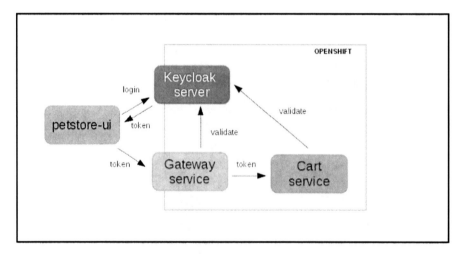

We will deploy the Keycloak service in our OpenShift cluster, and configure both customer gateway and **Cart service** so that they allow only users who can authorize as customers to use this part of the API. Let's start.

Installing Keycloak

In order to use Keycloak, we have to install it first. Keycloak is basically a Java application based on WildFly AS. For the purpose of cloud usage, an OpenShift Docker image is provided:

```
jboss/keycloak-openshift
```

The server has been configured in a way that enables it to be deployed directly to the OpenShift cluster. Let's use the OpenShift web console to deploy it:

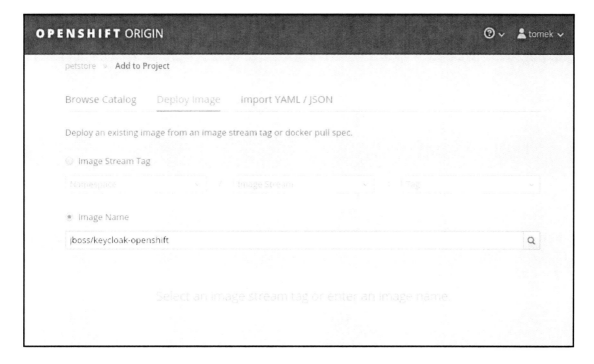

As we will see shortly, all the configuration will be performed using an admin console. In the configuration, we have to provide the initial admin credentials using **Environment Variables**:

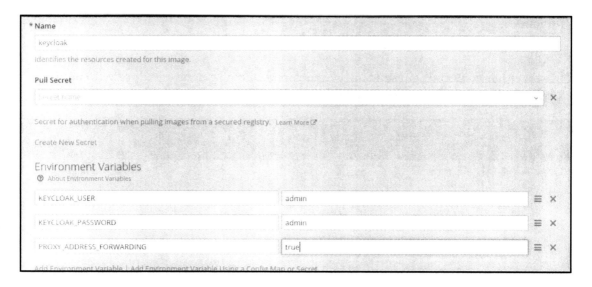

Since the server will be available behind the OpenShift proxy, we have to set the PROXY_ADDRESS_FORWARDING **parameter to** true.

After setting these parameters, we are ready to start deploying the image into our OpenShift cluster. We will need to click on the **Create** button and wait until the Keycloak pod starts.

Keycloak server, as with gateway servers, has to be accessed from outside the cluster (by us, administrators, and `petstore-ui`). Let's make a route, then. We will do this as in previous chapters: we have to click on **Create a route** in the **Services** menu of the web console. We should use the default parameters. After the route is created, we will be able to see its IP address, as follows:

Take a note of this IP, as we will use it quite a bit in a configuration.

OK, we have deployed Keycloak inside our cluster. We are finally ready to take a route to the Keycloak web console (the one that we have just created).

Creating realm

If you followed the created route, you will see the Keycloak welcome page. Click on the `Authentication console` link and enter the credentials that we defined when the Keycloak server was deployed to the cluster (**admin/admin**). You will see the **Admin** console.

The **Admin** console is a UI that allows you to easily configure all aspects of distributed security:

In the preceding screenshot, look at the top-left corner—the menu is titled **Master**. What does that mean? Keycloak is responsible for managing a group of users, their credentials, and roles and clients to whom users can delegate access to. Keycloak provides namespaces, which allow the grouping of those objects. Those namespaces are called **realms**. Realms are isolated, and each realm can only manage the objects that it contains. As a result, all services that communicate with the Keycloak server must specify which realm they are referring to.

For our purpose, we will create our own petstore realm. In order to do this, we have to click on **Master** in the top-left corner and add the new domain, called petstore.

Create a client

As mentioned in the theoretical section, the authentication server must be aware of all the clients that user can delegate their access to. In case of our application, we will need to configure a client: petstore-ui. In order to do this, click on **Clients** in the left-hand side menu and click on the **Create client** button:

We have to set the new client setting `Client ID` to `petstore-ui`. Remember that our web application will be redirected to Keycloak whenever a login is attempted. After the operation is finished, the authentication server has to redirect the user to the client using the redirect URI sent with the request by the client. Keycloak validates whether the URI is trusted. As a result, we have to provide a list of URI on which the client may be run. We will add the localhost address to which the browser with the UI is running. Also, some browsers perform **Cross-Origin Resource Sharing (CORS)** policy check. Setting the **Web Origins** parameter to + will make Keycloak return appropriate CORS headers with the redirect URI, if it was validated correctly.

We have now created our realm and told Keycloak about the client that will use it. Let's configure users now.

Users and roles

For the sake of this example, we will configure a user with **customer** and admin roles. Let's start with creating the roles themselves.

In the Keycloak console, we will need to click on **Roles** in the left-hand menu, click on the **Add role** button on the right-hand, and enter the **customer** role:

Next, we will need to repeat the preceding steps for the admin role.

Later, we will need to add the user in a similar way: click on the **Users** menu, then on the **Add user** button, and enter the name of our user:

This time, we have to perform more configuration though. We have to create the password in the **Credentials** section, as follows:

Then, map the **customer** role to the user:

We have created the user **tomek**, and given them **customer** and **admin** roles. If **tomek** uses `petstore-ui`, should they be able to invoke request allowed for admin roles? No. The `petstore-ui` is meant to be used by shop customers. We mentioned in the theoretical section that the authentication server should create an access token that contains the minimal amount of permissions necessary for the client do their job. In this concrete example, `petstore-ui` should only be allowed to perform a request allowed for customers on behalf of **tomek**. In order to configure that, we will need to introduce scopes.

Scopes

Keycloak scope is a tool that allows you to specify which roles will be associated with an access token generated for a specific client. Let's create a scope for the `pestore-ui` client.

In order to do this, you have to click on **Clients** in the left-hand side menu, choose the **petstore-ui** client, and click on the **Scope** tab below the client's name:

As you will have noticed in the preceding screenshot, each client has the full scope allowed parameter set to true by default. This means that each role that an authenticated user has will be associated with an access token created for that client. In order to limit the roles of the given client, we have to turn this option off and manually choose the roles that are allowed. In our example, we will need to choose the **customer** role and move it to assigned roles.

The **admin** role has not been moved. As a result, if an access token is generated for petstore-ui on behalf of **tomek**, it will only contain the **customer** role. As a result, **tomek** won't be able to perform any admin operations from within the petstore-ui client.

We have pretty much configured Keycloak.

So, how do you configure the Java services? Before finding that out, let's introduce the next functionality that requires user authentication—the cart service.

Cart service

Let's introduce the cart service implementation. First of all, we have to add the new resources to the customer-gateway API.

Examples reference: chapter10/cart-service

```
package org.packt.swarm.petstore;

import org.packt.swarm.petstore.api.CartItemView;
import org.packt.swarm.petstore.api.CatalogItemView;
import org.packt.swarm.petstore.cart.api.CartItem;

import javax.inject.Inject;
import javax.ws.rs.DELETE;
import javax.ws.rs.GET;
import javax.ws.rs.POST;
import javax.ws.rs.Path;
import javax.ws.rs.PathParam;
import javax.ws.rs.Produces;
import javax.ws.rs.QueryParam;
import javax.ws.rs.core.Context;
import javax.ws.rs.core.MediaType;
```

```
import javax.ws.rs.core.Response;
import javax.ws.rs.core.SecurityContext;
import java.util.List;

@Path("/")
public class GatewayResource {

    @Inject
    private GatewayService gatewayService;

    @GET
    @Path("/catalog/item")
    @Produces(MediaType.APPLICATION_JSON)
    public Response getItems() {
        List<CatalogItemView> result = gatewayService.getItems();
        return Response.ok(result).build();
    }

    @GET
    @Path("/cart/{customerId}")
    @Produces(MediaType.APPLICATION_JSON)
    public Response getCart(@PathParam("customerId") String customerId) {
        List<CartItemView> cart = gatewayService.getCart(customerId);
        return Response.ok(cart).build();
    }

    @POST
    @Path("/cart/{customerId}")
    @Produces(MediaType.APPLICATION_JSON)
    public Response addToCart(@PathParam("customerId") String customerId,
CartItem item, @QueryParam("additive") boolean additive) {
        gatewayService.addToCart(customerId, item, additive);
        return Response.ok().build();
    }

    @DELETE
    @Path("/cart/{customerId}/{itemId}")
    @Produces(MediaType.APPLICATION_JSON)
    public Response deleteFromCart(@PathParam("customerId") String
customerId, @PathParam("itemId") String itemId) {
        gatewayService.deleteFromCart(customerId, itemId);
        return Response.ok().build();
    }
    @POST
    @Path("payment")
    @Produces(MediaType.APPLICATION_JSON)
    public Response payment(@QueryParam("customerId") int customerId,
@Context  SecurityContext securityContext){
```

```
        try {
            String paymentUUID = gatewayService.buy(customerId);
            return Response.ok(paymentUUID).build();
        } catch (Exception e) {
            return Response.status(Response.Status.BAD_REQUEST).build();
        }
    }

}
```

As you will have noticed in the preceding code, we have added three cart methods. All of them identify the cart by `customerId` (we will show you how to obtain this in few moments) and the cart item using the `itemId` of the application. As in previous chapters, all the methods delegate the implementation to the gateway service, which in turn uses proxies to propagate the invocation to backend services.

In order to perform operations on the cart, a user has to be authenticated to the system. Let's secure the `GatewayResource` to make sure that an unauthorized user will be denied access to those methods.

WildFly Swarm Keycloak adapter

As you will know from the theoretical section, services with a secured API will have to authorize their users based on authentication tokens. In order to do that, they have to cooperate with the Keycloak server using, in our example, the OIDC protocol. Obviously, we will not implement this functionality ourselves. As we've suggested, Keycloak provides a number of adapters for different tools. WildFly Swarm has its own adapter too. So, how will we install it?

Let's extend customer-gateway's `pom.xml`:

```
(...)
<dependency>
    <groupId>org.wildfly.swarm</groupId>
    <artifactId>keycloak</artifactId>
    <version>${version.wildfly.swarm}</version>
</dependency>
(...)
```

That's it—the adapter is installed.

We have one more thing to do. We have to configure the adapter. In order to do this, we have to add the `keycloak.json` file inside the Maven's resources directory. The file contains a bunch of adapter configuration properties. In our case, it's pretty simple:

```
{
    "realm": "petstore",
    "auth-server-url": "${env.KEYCLOAK_URL}/auth",
    "resource": "petstore-ui"
}
```

Basically, the files tell the adapter the `auth-server`'s location, the realm, and the resource name. As you may recall, we were behind all of those: we created the route to the Keycloak server deployed on OpenShift, created the realm for our petstore application, and told Keycloak that we will authenticate using the `petstore-ui` client, which we configured.

Please, note that we need to provide KEYCLOAK_URL as an environment variable. This is an URL of the keycloak proxy that we have created. You are able to configure this variable in the web-console:

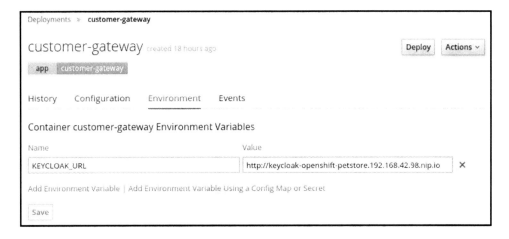

After this information is provided, the Keycloak adapter will be able to authorize users based on the access token provided by the UI. This is good, but we haven't protected our resources yet.

In order to do this, we have to introduce few changes to customer-gateway's main class:

```
package org.packt.swarm.petstore;

import org.jboss.shrinkwrap.api.Archive;
import org.wildfly.swarm.Swarm;
import org.wildfly.swarm.keycloak.Secured;

public class Main {

    public static void main(String[] args) throws Exception {
        (...)
        Archive<?> deployment = swarm.createDefaultDeployment();
        secureDeployment(deployment);

        swarm.deploy(deployment);
    }

    private static void secureDeployment(final Archive<?> deployment){
        deployment.as(Secured.class)
                .protect("/cart/*")
                .withMethod("POST","GET","DELETE")
                .withRole("customer");
    }
}
```

As you will have noticed in the preceding code, after marking deployment as Secured, we are able to use a chained API that we use to specify which request on which resources to protect and which roles are allowed.

With the preceding code, we have made sure that only users with the customer role is able to use cart-associated methods in the customer API. Note, however, that the backend cart service has to be secured as well.

We will secure it to the gateway service in an analogous way, which makes sure that it has dependency on swarm's Keycloak adapter, adding keycloak.json to the classpath (note that the context of the file will be the same, as all the properties stay valid), and making deployment secure in the main function.

We have one problem though: in the gateway service, we have relied on the UI to send us access token each time the request is performed by an authenticated user. As you may recall from the previous chapters, we use Rest Client to perform the invocation on the backend service, and are responsible for attaching all the necessary information. As a result, we also have to propagate the access token to backend services during the invocation. If we don't do this, Keycloak adapter in the backend service will recognize the request being performed as anonymous, which is clearly invalid.

In order to propagate the context, we will implement a simple JAX-RS client request filter. In our scenario, we will check whether the access token is present and, if true, propagate it further to the invocation:

```
package org.packt.swarm.petstore.security;

import org.keycloak.KeycloakPrincipal;

import javax.ws.rs.client.ClientRequestContext;
import javax.ws.rs.client.ClientRequestFilter;
import javax.ws.rs.core.Context;
import javax.ws.rs.core.HttpHeaders;
import javax.ws.rs.core.SecurityContext;
import javax.ws.rs.ext.Provider;
import java.io.IOException;

//1
public class AuthTokenPropagationFilter implements ClientRequestFilter {

    private static final String BEARER = "Bearer";

    //2
    @Context
    SecurityContext securityContext;

    @Override
    public void filter(ClientRequestContext requestContext) throws
IOException {
        //3
        KeycloakPrincipal keycloakPrincipal = (KeycloakPrincipal)
securityContext.getUserPrincipal();
        //4
        if(keycloakPrincipal != null &&
keycloakPrincipal.getKeycloakSecurityContext()!=null) {
            //5
            String token =
keycloakPrincipal.getKeycloakSecurityContext().getTokenString();
            if(token != null) {
```

```
            //6
                requestContext.getHeaders().add(HttpHeaders.AUTHORIZATION,
    BEARER + " " + token);
                }
            }
        }
    }
```

Let's analyze this code step by step:

1. As you may recall, JAX-RS `ClientRequestFilter` (1) filters every invocation performed by the client associated with it before it is propagated to the server. In our scenario, we will check whether the access token is present and attach it to each request if true.
2. In (2), we are injecting the `SecurityContext`. If Keycloak has authorized the user using the access token, it creates the `SecurityContext` and attaches it to the request. As a result, we will inject it into the objects on the invocation thread.
3. The `SecurityContext` created by Keycloak contains the `KeycloakPrincipal` implementation of the principal interface (3).
4. If the principal is present, we will be able to obtain further `KeycloakSecurityContext` from it (5).
5. Finally, the token can be obtained from the context and propagated further as a BEARER token.

Let's look at `CartProxy` now:

```java
package org.packt.swarm.petstore.proxy;

import org.packt.swarm.petstore.cart.api.CartItem;
import org.packt.swarm.petstore.security.AuthTokenPropagationFilter;

import javax.annotation.PostConstruct;
import javax.enterprise.context.ApplicationScoped;
import javax.ws.rs.client.Client;
import javax.ws.rs.client.ClientBuilder;
import javax.ws.rs.client.Entity;
import javax.ws.rs.client.WebTarget;
import javax.ws.rs.core.MediaType;
import java.util.Arrays;
import java.util.List;

@ApplicationScoped
public class CartProxy {
```

```
    (...)

    public List<org.packt.swarm.petstore.cart.api.CartItem> getCart(String
customerId){
            Client client = ClientBuilder.newClient();
            client.register(new AuthTokenPropagationFilter());
            WebTarget target = client.target(targetPath + "/cart/" +
customerId);
            return
Arrays.asList(target.request(MediaType.APPLICATION_JSON).get(org.packt.swar
m.petstore.cart.api.CartItem[].class));
    }

    (...)

}
```

The proxy is similar to the proxies that we created in previous chapters and uses the standard JAX-RS client API to create an appropriate request to the backend cart-service. However, we have to register the TokenPropagationFilter that we have just created for the client

Let's sum up what we have already done: we have extended the customer-gateway with cart methods, added a Keycloak adapter and its configuration to the project, and marked deployment as Secured, specifying the roles that are authorized to use the given methods. We did this for both customer-gateway and backend cart-service. In order to make sure that the access token is propagated to the backend service, we have implemented an appropriate filter and registered it inside our proxy. It seems that the authentication should work now. Let's try it!

 You are going to find UI application in the attached code: chapter10/petstore-ui.

Let's start the petstore application and open the UI:

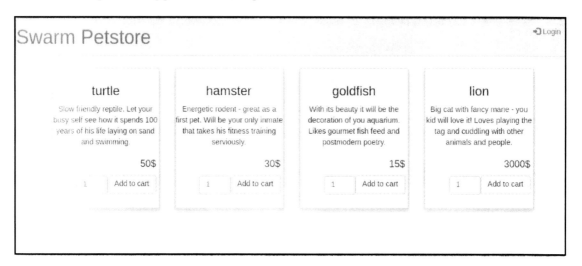

In the preceding screenshot, no user is logged in to the application. To obtain all the necessary data, the client had to perform the invocation on the items resource. As the resource is not protected, the invocation was successful. In order to log in to the cart, we have to be authenticated. Let's do it:

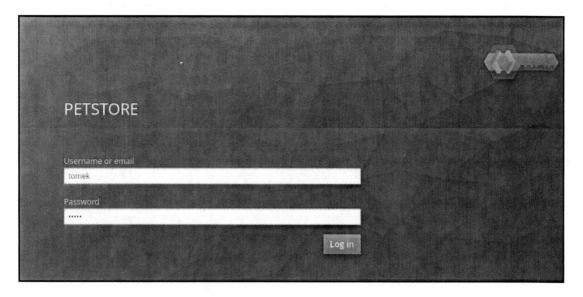

Clicking on the **Log in** button redirected us to Keycloak server. After providing your credentials, Keycloak will authenticate you and redirect you to the store:

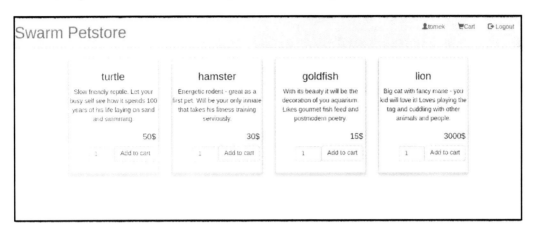

As you will have noticed in the preceding screenshot, we have successfully logged in to the UI. You can now add items to the cart and take a look at the cart view:

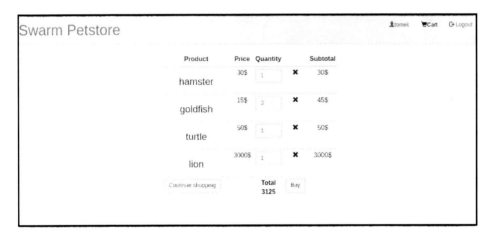

We have shown you the operation of the store with a valid security configuration, but feel free to play with the sample application in order to confirm that the security works correctly. You may create and remove roles from the user in the Keycloak console, or make the service require different roles for authorization. You will see that Keycloak is indeed able to correctly authorize a user; users with valid roles will be allowed to perform a request and users lacking valid roles will be forbidden.

SSL configuration

As we mentioned at the beginning of this chapter, when we describe bearer tokens, when you use this kind of authentication in a production environment, you have to use encrypted connections. In this section, we will describe how WildFly Swarm and OpenShift support the use of secure connections.

We will separate this section into two different cases, depending on whether we consider our cloud environment to be secured or not.

Secured cloud

In a scenario where the cloud environment that you are using is secure, you will need to configure an encrypted connection between external clients and routers:

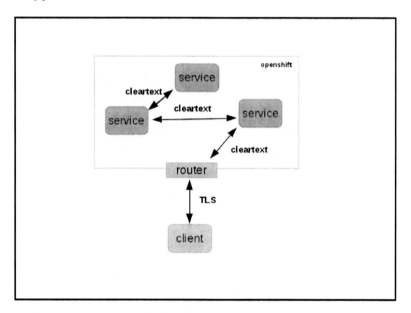

In such a case, we have to configure an **Edge** router. An **Edge** router has its own certificate and is able to establish secure connections with external clients. Before proxying traffic to the destination, the router encrypts the connection. As a result, in the OpenShift cluster, communication happens through unsecured connections.

You are able to configure edge routing for each route that you create. In order to do so, you have to create routes in the standard way (choose the service to which you want the route to be established and click on **Create route**). Later, you have to choose a **Secure route** so, pick **Edge** from the **TLS termination** drop-down menu and enter your **Certificate** in the PEM format in the form, as follows:

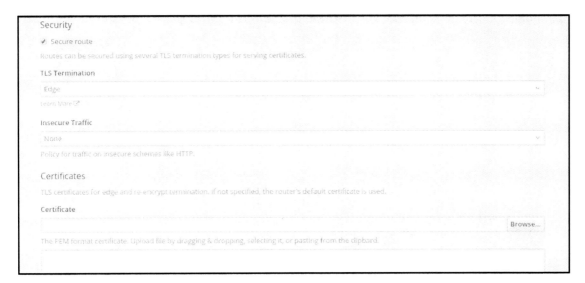

Unsecured cloud

In some circumstances, you may need to configure secure connections for all communication, both with external services and within the cloud:

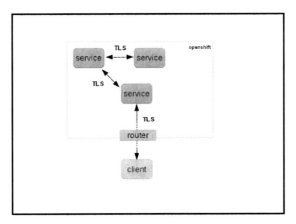

In order to do so, you have to configure a route with passthrough TLS termination (by creating the route in the same way as in the paragraph before and choosing pass-through termination).

With the pass-through termination, the router does not terminate the TLS connection and the encrypted traffic is propagated to the target. One of its implications is that targets (and all other services) need to have their security setting configured.

Swarm enables you to do this easily by providing HTTP configuration. Let's look at the example configuration:

```
swarm:
  https:
    only: true
    port: 8443
  http:
    keystore:
      path: keystore.jks
      password: password
    truststore:
      path: truststore.jks
      password: password
```

The preceding configuration specifies that the server will only use the secured connection on the 8443 port. It specifies the location of both `trustore` and `keystore` (classpath) and their `passwords`.

Summary

In this chapter, we've shown how you can use distributed security protocols to secure your cloud applications using our practical example.

We started this chapter by introducing concepts based on distributed authentication and authorization: the rationale for tokens and how they can be obtained and used. Later, we introduced basic information about a concrete distributed security protocol: OpenID Connect.

In the practical section, we used the Keycloak SSO server to secure the cart service in the Petstore application.

In the, we will discuss how do deal with an unreliable network problem using a circuit breaker pattern; specifically, the Hystrix library.

Further reading

1. `https://oauth.net/2/`
2. `http://openid.net/developers/specs/`
3. `https://www.keycloak.org/`

11
Adding Resilience Using Hystrix

In this chapter, we will learn how to deal with network failures, which are inevitable in a distributed environment. In order to do that, we will introduce the **circuit breaker** architectural pattern and cover when it should be used, and what its benefits are. We will look at its Netflix implementation, **Hystrix**. We will also cover how it is implemented and how it can be used. As an example, we will use Hystrix to add resilience and fault tolerance to our sample application.

Unreliable network

When you develop your services for distributed environments, you must take into consideration that invocations of the services will be performed over the network. As a result, the application must be prepared to deal with network failures, which will certainly happen.

This problem is further enhanced by the fact that a single misbehaving service can poison a large number of services. Let's take a look at the number of scenarios, that can make this possible.

Dependent services

In large distributed systems, each service would have a large number of dependencies on other services. It requires only one dependency to fail to make the service irresponsible. Also, a service will go down too, becoming unavailable for other services that depend on it. Such a situation is known as cascading failures (Further reading, link 1).

However, that's not all. In a production-ready environment when there are a lot of calls being performed, a service that has latency problems will quickly block all available threads and make all other services unreachable.

Clearly, if we want to design a robust distributed system, we will need to have a tool that will enable users to deal with the problems described previously. The tool that we will use is the Hystrix library.

Hystrix is a library developed by Netflix to deal with service failures and to provide robustness for its sophisticated distributed architecture. Let's find out how Hystrix deals with the problems previously described.

The circuit breaker pattern

The architectural design pattern created to deal with the problems described previously is the circuit breaker pattern. The main idea behind it is simple: wrap the invocation code into the command, which will perform the invocation, and calculate the status of the remote service. If the service is declared unreachable by the metrics used by the command, then the next invocations are rejected immediately. After a given time, new connections will be tried again, and, if successful, the command will start performing invocations to the service again.

The name of the pattern was taken from the electrical circuit breaker, a device used to protect the electrical circuit from the damage that may result from the excess electrical current. If the current in the circuit is too high then the circuit breaker opens, preventing the current from flowing. In order to make the circuit operate again, the circuit breaker has to be closed.

Owing to its archetype, the software circuit breaker has inherited the electrical nomenclature. If the targeted service is healthy and the invocations are forwarded to it directly, we will be talking about closed breaker. If the health metrics are exceed, the invocations are not performed, and the circuit breaker will be opened.

Obviously, the library that is responsible for the implementation of the circuit breaker has to provide algorithms that decide whether the remote service is healthy, how and when to open the circuit, and what to do if a circuit breaker is closed. Let's discuss how Hystrix does it.

The Hystrix circuit breaker

The following diagram presents the behavior of the Hystrix circuit breaker:

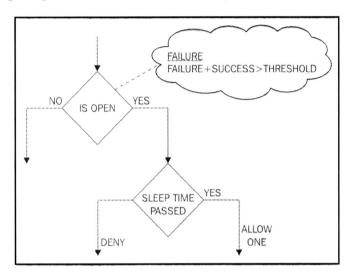

During the invocation of the remote service, Hystrix checks whether the circuit breaker is open. This decision is made based on the statistics gathered from the recent invocations. If the percentage of failures in the last time window is lower than the configured threshold, then the circuit is open and the invocation is performed.

After the invocation is performed, the circuit breaker stores its result (success/failure) in the statistics. The statistics are gathered for the configured time window, which is further divided into the number of buckets, with only one bucket being discarded at a time so that the data for the given window is not discarded all at once.

What happens when the circuit is open? Firstly, the algorithm checks whether the configured sleep time has passed. If it is the case, then only one request is allowed to be executed. This stage of a circuit breaker is called half-open and its purpose is to check whether the invoked service is healthy again. If the invocation succeeds, then a circuit breaker is opened again and the metrics are reset. If, on the other hand, the sleep time has not exceeded or the one invocation in a half-open state has failed, then the circuit breaker is opened again and the sleep time is reset.

So, we now know the Hystrix circuit breaker algorithm and how it reacts to statistics on successful and failed invocation. However, how do we actually define failure? There are three cases when the invocation is marked as failed. First, the configured invocation timeout has been exceeded. Second, the client library has thrown an exception. Third, the number of threads available for a given dependency has been exceeded.

The last point is an implementation of the bulkheading algorithm. Let's learn more about it.

Bulkheading

In order to prevent a situation in which one of the dependencies uses the whole thread pool of an application, Hystrix keeps the thread pool for each dependency. If one of the dependencies becomes latent, it will keep all its threads busy and will reject further invocations, resulting in an increased failure count. Such a strategy is called **bulkheading**.

This time, the nomenclature is taken from ship engineering: the hull of the ship is divided into isolated bulkheads so that the hull damage in one place results in only one bulkhead being filled with water. Similarly, providing a thread pool for each of the dependencies results in only a dedicated thread pool being used if one of the services is misbehaving.

In complex distributed environments, it is often the case that the application has many dependencies, each of which depends on other client libraries. Often, such libraries are black boxes provided by a third-party company, making them hard to debug. In addition, increasing the number of those libraries increases the risk that one of them will *poison* the whole application. With bulkheading, you can easily mitigate this risk.

 The state of each client can be easily tracked by the status of its thread pool. If monitoring shows that one of the thread pools is full, it is an indicator that it should be examined. If the underlying problem is fixed, the thread pool will clear up and the service will continue its operation.

The dependencies that share the same thread pool are configurable. As a result, you are able to tune bulkheading behavior according to your architecture. Such a configuration is done using Hystrix group mechanism, which we will show you in the examples later in this chapter.

So, we already know that the invocation may fail or be forced to fail by Hystrix. But, what happens in that scenario? The mechanism that is supposed to deal with invocation failures is called **fallbacks**. Let's learn more about it now.

Fallbacks

Hystrix implements a fallbacks mechanism, which allows you to execute your code whenever the failure of the invocation happens. The command allows you to implement a fallback method, which will be executed during the failure. The method is executed regardless of the cause of the failure—the same method will be executed in case of timeout or thread pool overflow.

The fallback method doesn't have to be implemented. If fallback is not implemented, the exception thrown by Hystrix will be propagated down the stack trace.

If, on the other hand, you decide to implement the fallback, you have a number of strategies for doing that. Let's take a look at a few examples.

If you are using a service that is used to read a data, you can return an empty answer in case of invocation failure. In such a scenario, no data will be available in case of service failure. This solution hides the underlying failure and immediately returns the response. The problem is, obviously, that the requested data is unavailable. You can deal with that by implementing the local cache and return the latest response in case of failure. In this scenario, the failure will be hidden and the data will be available. It won't be up to date for the time of failure, but it will allow your system to continue its operation.

Let's suppose now that you are using the authorization service to decide whether the user is authorized to perform some further operations. In this case, you can implement the fallback, which will always return the same response. However, what should this response be? As usual, it depends on your use case. In some scenarios, you may want to avoid a situation when a user who has paid for a service is unable to use it. In this scenario, you would return the successful authorization each time. The drawback is that a number of users will be able to use content that they haven't paid for at the time of authorization service failure. In other scenarios, you may need to deny authorization for all users. Surely the temporary allow-all strategy is not suitable for the bank application. In this case, you would have to deny the authorization for all users.

Finally, in some scenarios, not writing the fallback is a good strategy. Let's suppose that you are implementing an invocation that is supposed to modify some data as a part of transactional operations. In this scenario, the propagated exception is the strategy that we want: the whole operation will be stopped, and the exception will be propagated to the transaction manager, which will roll back the transaction.

In this section, we have only hinted at a number of possible fallback implementation strategies. As you may have noticed, the specific implementation (or lack of) depends directly on your service's business requirements. The key point to remember is that Hystrix won't allow the network failure to compromise the behavior of your application, and if a failure occurs it will allow you to deal with it using the fallback mechanism.

The whole algorithm

Finally, we are ready to sum up the behavior of the Hystrix library:

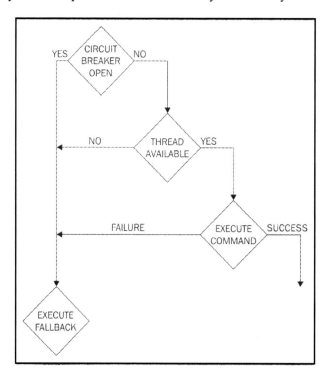

At the beginning, the user constructs the command and starts its execution. Hystrix checks whether the circuit breaker associated with this command is closed. If the circuit breaker is open, then the invocation will be rejected immediately and the fallback will be executed (if implemented). If the circuit breaker is closed, then the thread-pool is checked. If there are no available threads in the thread-pool, then the invocation fails; optionally, the fallback is executed and the failure is reported to the circuit breaker. If, on the other hand, there are threads available, then the invocation starts. If the invocation misses its timeout, then the failure is reported to the circuit breaker and the optional fallback is executed.

In this scenario, the thread may be blocked. Hystrix will time it out, but will have to wait for the client library to *return the thread*. If the invocation finishes and fails, then the failure is reported to the circuit breaker and optionally the fallback is executed.

Finally, if the execution succeeds, then the success is reported to the circuit breaker and the response is returned as the result of the command execution.

You have already learned the basics of the Hystrix's circuit breaker implementation. Now it is time to learn its basic API, which we will use later in this chapter. Let's do it now.

Using Hystrix

In order to learn Hystrix behavior in practice, we are going to extend customer-gateway service so that it uses Hystrix for its invocations. Later, we are going to make one of our services artificially unresponsive and see how Hystrix behaves. Let's start.

Examples reference: `chapter11/customer-gateway-hystrix`.

Firstly, we are going to add Hystrix dependency to the `pom.xml`:

```
(...)

<dependency>
    <groupId>com.netflix.hystrix</groupId>
    <artifactId>hystrix-core</artifactId>
    <version>${version.hystrix}</version>
</dependency>

(...)
```

The circuit breaker command is implemented by extending the `com.netflix.hystrix.HystrixCommand` class. Let's take a look at its usage at the concrete example of our `PricingProxy`:

```
(...)

@ApplicationScoped
public class PricingProxy {
```

```
(...)

//1
private class GetPriceCommand extends HystrixCommand<Response> {

    private final String itemId;

    //2
    public GetPriceCommand(String itemId) {
        //3
super(Setter.withGroupKey(HystrixCommandGroupKey.Factory.asKey("pricing-
service"));
        this.itemId = itemId;
    }

    @Override
    //4
    protected Response run() {
        //5
        Client client = ClientBuilder.newClient();
        WebTarget target = client.target(targetPath + "/price/" +
itemId);
        return target.request(MediaType.APPLICATION_JSON).get();
    }
  }
}
```

The command has to extend the abstract HystrixCommand class (1). The class has to be parameterized with a type that will be returned as the command result. In our example, it will be the JAX-RS response class—the same as we used in our raw invocation.

The class takes the itemId parameter as an argument (2), which will be used in the invocation.

As you can see in the constructor code, we have provided HystrixCommandGroupKey parameter to it (3). HystrixCommand constructors allow you to provide a combination of three arguments: HystrixCommandGroupKey, HystrixThreadPoolKey, and the timeout. The two enum parameters are used for command grouping: the commands with the same group key will belong to the same group and will be grouped together for the purpose of reporting, alerting, and monitoring. The thread pool key specifies the commands that belong to the same Hystrix thread pool used by the bulkhead algorithm. When the thread pool key is not enabled, the group key is used as the thread pool identifier.

As a result, in our example all the `pricingService` invocation commands will belong to the same group and will use their own thread pool. The third argument in the `HystrixCommand` constructors is the timeout of the invocation. If one is not provided, the default timeout is used.

We have to extend the `run` method of the HystrixCommand class (4). This method will be invoked when the command is executed. As you can see (5), the content of the method is the same as the code of the proxy in our raw invocation.

Now, let's take a look at how to execute the command:

```
(...)

@ApplicationScoped
public class PricingProxy {

    private final String targetPath =
System.getProperty("proxy.pricing.url");
    //1
    public Price getPrice(String itemId){
        //2
        return new
GetPriceCommand(itemId).execute().readEntity(Price.class);
    }

    (...)
}
```

The getPrice method of the proxy (1) creates the command object (2) and invokes the `execute()` method on it. This results in the execution of the whole circuit breaker algorithm described in the theoretical section. Let's invoke the catalog/item method now and measure the time of its invocation:

```
[tomek@localhost ~]$ time curl -X GET http://customer-gateway-petstore.192.168.42.48.nip.io/cata
log/item
[{"itemId":"dbf67f4d-f1c9-4fd4-96a8-65ee1a22b9ff","name":"turtle","quantity":5,"price":50,"descr
iption":"Slow friendly reptile. Let your busy self see how it spends 100 years of his life layin
g on sand and swimming."},{"itemId":"fc7ee3ea-8f82-4144-bcc8-9a71f4d871bd","name":"hamster","qua
ntity":10,"price":30,"description":"Energetic rodent - great as a first pet. Will be your only i
nmate that takes his fitness training serviously."},{"itemId":"725dfad2-0b4d-455c-9385-b46c9f356
e9b","name":"goldfish","quantity":3,"price":15,"description":"With its beauty it will be the dec
oration of you aquarium. Likes gourmet fish feed and postmodern poetry."},{"itemId":"a2aa1ca7-ad
d8-4aae-b361-b7f92d82c3f5","name":"lion","quantity":9,"price":3000,"description":"Loves playing
the tag and cuddling with other animals and people."}]
real    0m0.133s
user    0m0.003s
sys     0m0.005s
[tomek@localhost ~]$
```

There is no difference; the invocation is executed immediately without any errors. Now, let's make pricingService artificially unresponsive.

 Examples reference: chapter11/pricing-service-misbehave.

In order to do that we are going to make the service wait a specified amount of time before returning a result:

```
package org.packt.swarm.petstore.pricing;

import org.packt.swarm.petstore.pricing.model.Price;

import javax.enterprise.context.ApplicationScoped;
import javax.persistence.EntityManager;
import javax.persistence.PersistenceContext;
import java.util.List;
import java.util.concurrent.TimeUnit;
import java.util.concurrent.locks.LockSupport;

@ApplicationScoped
public class PricingService {

    @PersistenceContext(unitName = "PricingPU")
    private EntityManager em;

    public Price findByItemId(String itemId) {
        //1
        LockSupport.parkNanos(TimeUnit.SECONDS.toNanos(5));
        return em.createNamedQuery("Price.findByItemId",
Price.class).setParameter("itemId", itemId).getSingleResult();
    }
}
```

Let's deploy the new service to the cloud and retry an invocation. The result is as follows:

```
[tomek@localhost ~]$ time curl -X GET http://customer-gateway-petstore.192.168.42.48.nip.io/catalog/item
<html><head><title>Error</title></head><body>Internal Server Error</body></html>
real    0m1.057s
user    0m0.004s
sys     0m0.005s
[tomek@localhost ~]$
```

As you will have noticed in the preceding screenshot, the invocation has resulted in failure. The circuit breaker was open, and there was a thread available in the thread pool. As a result, the invocation was performed, but it exceeded the default Hystrix timeout which equals 1 second.

To confirm this, let's look at the logs:

```
Caused by: com.netflix.hystrix.exception.HystrixRuntimeException: GetPriceCommand timed-out and no fallback available.
    at com.netflix.hystrix.AbstractCommand$22.call(AbstractCommand.java:819)
    at com.netflix.hystrix.AbstractCommand$22.call(AbstractCommand.java:804)
    at rx.internal.operators.OperatorOnErrorResumeNextViaFunction$4.onError(OperatorOnErrorResumeNextViaFunction.java:140)
    at rx.internal.operators.OnSubscribeDoOnEach$DoOnEachSubscriber.onError(OnSubscribeDoOnEach.java:87)
    at rx.internal.operators.OnSubscribeDoOnEach$DoOnEachSubscriber.onError(OnSubscribeDoOnEach.java:87)
    at com.netflix.hystrix.AbstractCommand$DeprecatedOnFallbackHookApplication$1.onError(AbstractCommand.java:1472)
    at com.netflix.hystrix.AbstractCommand$FallbackHookApplication$1.onError(AbstractCommand.java:1397)
```

Hystrix does not lie here: the timeout was exceeded and we have implemented no fallback. We will do in a second, but before that let's learn how to modify Hystrix properties.

If you want to modify the configuration of `HystrixCommand`, you have to use the constructor with the `Setter` argument. This class allows you to configure all the constructor arguments described previously. Apart from that, the class allows you to provide the configuration properties for different aspects of the circuit breaker behavior. The exhaustive list of such properties is described in the Hystrix documentation. Here, we will present a few example modifications. Let's start with the circuit breaker timeout:

```
(...)
private class GetPriceCommand extends HystrixCommand<Response> {

    private final String itemId;

    public GetPriceCommand(String itemId) {
        //1
super(Setter.withGroupKey(HystrixCommandGroupKey.Factory.asKey("pricing-
service"))
.andCommandPropertiesDefaults(HystrixCommandProperties.Setter()
        //2
                        .withExecutionTimeoutInMilliseconds(100)));
        this.itemId = itemId;
    }

    @Override
    protected Response run() {
        Client client = ClientBuilder.newClient();
        WebTarget target = client.target(targetPath + "/price/" + itemId);
```

```
            return target.request(MediaType.APPLICATION_JSON).get();
        }
    }
    (...)
```

The preceding code modifies our command class in order to shorten the invocation timeout to 500 milliseconds. The `Setter` class is used, and the `CommandGroupKey` is set in the same way as in the examples before (1). In order to modify the configuration, we have added `HystrixCommandProperites.Setter` with the appropriate configuration (2). Now, let's take a look at the following result:

```
[tomek@localhost ~]$ time curl -X GET http://customer-gateway-petstore.192.168.42.48.nip.io/cata
log/item
<html><head><title>Error</title></head><body>Internal Server Error</body></html>
real    0m0.174s
user    0m0.004s
sys     0m0.004s
[tomek@localhost ~]$
```

Let's reconfigure the application to note the behavior of the bulkheading algorithm; we will increase the timeout and reduce the number of threads:

```
(...)private class GetPriceCommand extends HystrixCommand<Response> {

    private final String itemId;

    public GetPriceCommand(String itemId) {
    super(Setter.withGroupKey(HystrixCommandGroupKey.Factory.asKey("pricing-
service"))
    //1
    .andThreadPoolPropertiesDefaults(HystrixThreadPoolProperties.Setter().withC
oreSize(3));
        this.itemId = itemId;
    }

    @Override
    protected Response run() {
        Client client = ClientBuilder.newClient();
        WebTarget target = client.target(targetPath + "/price/" + itemId);
        return target.request(MediaType.APPLICATION_JSON).get();
    }
}
(...)
```

In order to do that, another setter (this time, the `HystrixThreadPoolProperties` setter) has to be created (1).

The result is as follows:

```
[tomek@localhost ~]$ time curl -X GET http://customer-gateway-petstore.192.168.42.48.nip.io/catalog/item &
[1] 6643
[tomek@localhost ~]$ time curl -X GET http://customer-gateway-petstore.192.168.42.48.nip.io/catalog/item &
[2] 6646
[tomek@localhost ~]$ time curl -X GET http://customer-gateway-petstore.192.168.42.48.nip.io/catalog/item &
[3] 6649
[tomek@localhost ~]$ time curl -X GET http://customer-gateway-petstore.192.168.42.48.nip.io/catalog/item &
[4] 6652
[tomek@localhost ~]$ <html><head><title>Error</title></head><body>Internal Server Error</body></html>
real    0m0.062s
user    0m0.007s
sys     0m0.004s
<html><head><title>Error</title></head><body>Internal Server Error</body></html>
real    0m1.302s
user    0m0.002s
sys     0m0.009s
<html><head><title>Error</title></head><body>Internal Server Error</body></html>
real    0m1.079s
user    0m0.003s
sys     0m0.003s
<html><head><title>Error</title></head><body>Internal Server Error</body></html>
real    0m1.070s
user    0m0.004s
sys     0m0.004s
```

As you will have noticed in the preceding screenshot, the first three invocations have obtained their threads and were blocked. The fourth thread returned immediately as there are no more threads in the thread pool.

Finally, let's open the circuit. If we run the code in a bash loop and look into the log, we will note the following result:

```
Caused by: java.lang.RuntimeException: Hystrix circuit short-circuited and is OPEN
        at com.netflix.hystrix.AbstractCommand.handleShortCircuitViaFallback(AbstractCommand.java:979)
        at com.netflix.hystrix.AbstractCommand.applyHystrixSemantics(AbstractCommand.java:557)
        at com.netflix.hystrix.AbstractCommand.access$200(AbstractCommand.java:60)
        at com.netflix.hystrix.AbstractCommand$4.call(AbstractCommand.java:419)
        at com.netflix.hystrix.AbstractCommand$4.call(AbstractCommand.java:413)
        at rx.internal.operators.OnSubscribeDefer.call(OnSubscribeDefer.java:46)
        ... 80 more
```

Finally, let's implement the fallback:

```
(...)
private class CreatePaymentCommand extends HystrixCommand<Response> {

    private final Payment payment;

    public CreatePaymentCommand(Payment payment) {
super(Setter.withGroupKey(HystrixCommandGroupKey.Factory.asKey(SERVICE_NAME
))
.andCommandPropertiesDefaults(HystrixCommandProperties.Setter()
.withExecutionTimeoutInMilliseconds(100)));
        this.payment = payment;
    }

    @Override
    protected Response run() {
        Client client = ClientBuilder.newClient();
        WebTarget target = client.target(targetPath + "/payment");
        return
target.request(MediaType.APPLICATION_JSON).post(Entity.json(payment));
    }

    @Override
    //1
    protected Response getFallback() {
        //2
        return
Response.status(Response.Status.SERVICE_UNAVAILABLE).build();
    }
}

(...)
```

In order to implement the fallback, you have to override the `getFallback` method (1). In our example, we have returned the `SERVICE_UNAVAILABLE` exception whenever the `paymentService` is unreachable (2).

We can now reimplement the `PetstoreService` so that it creates a meaningful exception whenever such situations occur:

```
public String buy(int customerId){
    Cart cart = cartProxy.getCart(customerId);

    Order order = createOrderFromCart(customerId, cart);
    int orderId = orderProxy.createOrder(order);
```

```
    Payment payment = new Payment();
    payment.setMerchantId(Constants.MERCHANT_ID);
    payment.setDescription(String.format("ORDER_ID: %s", orderId));
    payment.setAmount(order.getPrice());

    Response response = paymentProxy.createPayment(payment);

    if(response.getStatus() ==
Response.Status.SERVICE_UNAVAILABLE.getStatusCode()){
        throw new RuntimeException("Payment service unreachable");
    }

    return (String) response.readEntity(String.class);
}
```

This will be the result of an invocation:

```
[tomek@localhost ~]$ curl -X GET http://customer-gateway-petstore.192.168.42.48.nip.io/catalog/item; echo
HTTP 503 Service Unavailable
[tomek@localhost ~]$ ▊
```

Summary

In this chapter, we covered the basic theory behind the circuit breaker pattern.

In the practical part of this chapter, we extended our pet store application to provide the buying functionality. We then covered the basics of the Hystrix API and used it to implement resilient connections with our external payment service.

Later, we used our own mock implementation of misbehaving a payment service to present the behavior of the circuit breaker algorithm.

Further reading

1. https://github.com/Netflix/Hystrix/wiki
2. http://netflix.github.io/Hystrix/javadoc/

12
Future Direction

In this chapter, we will describe briefly what the future of Java EE development is likely to look like—what the plans of evolving the platform are and how concepts provided by applications described in the book may be standardized in the future. We will also take a look at MicroProfile and Jakarta EE projects—describe their purpose, and emphasize how it can help you to move the platform forward at a faster pace.

In the first chapter, we have sketched the process in which Java EE standard is being created, emphasizing the benefits it provides: portability and interoperability. It seems that, in order to keep it up with the IT pace, we've had to abandon those benefits. Let's take a look at this problem more thoroughly.

No more standards?

Having a number of tools that allow us to immediately take advantage of modern software architectures has made our life easier. These tools have emerged during recent years in order to deal with the problems that have to be solved when building systems consisting of a large number of ephemeral services distributed across the network. It has to be noted that, although we have chosen the proven solutions such as Hystrix or Keycloak, we have lost the mentioned portability and interoperability benefits of Java EE.

The problem was that the process in which the Java EE standard was being created wasn't able to keep up with the rapid pace of the development of the emerging technologies. The specifications that provide a common standard for solving problems associated with cloud architecture (for example, distributed security or network resilience) are not yet a part of Java EE. What are the reasons for that?

The pace at which recent versions of the standard were created was too slow to follow all the recent innovations: Java EE 7 was released in 2013, whereas Java EE 8 was released in 2017. This is not the only problem though. The specifications are designed according to the Java Community Process. The process is meticulous and contains a number of steps that are supposed to make sure that the resulting standard is ready to be published.

This process works well when you are indeed standardizing—extracting the knowledge accumulated by the industry in order to provide common APIs to solve a problem in a proven way. On the other hand, it is not so good for innovation. If solutions to a given problem emerge, the creators of the specification have to effectively guess the correct solution. This is very hard no matter how meticulous the standard process is.

So, should we abandon all the standards after all, in order to follow the innovation? Put it another way; is losing standard benefits of portability, interoperability, and longtime support an inevitable consequence of the pace at which the current IT world is moving? Maybe we can do better than that. Let's discuss Eclipse MicroProfile.

Eclipse MicroProfile

Eclipse MicroProfile is a project that defines a programming model for developing Java microservices (Further reading, link 1). Similar to the Java EE standard, it contains a number of specifications that define the common way to provide functionalities needed by the
`microservices`.

Let's take a look at the current content of the project (version 2.0):

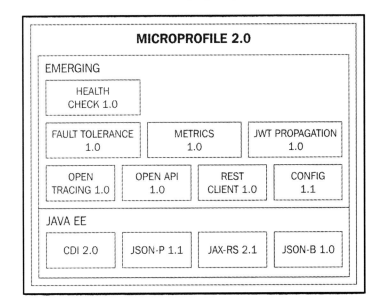

As you will have noticed in the preceding diagram, there are a bunch of specifications that have come directly from Java EE, and that we have used extensively in our examples throughout the book (for example, JAX-RS or CDI). However, there are also a number of novel specifications that are supposed to deal with microservices-specific problems. As an example, the JWT Propagation specification deals with token-based security, and fault tolerance deals with the network failures.

As you are able to see, MicroProfile is an emerging project that will allow you to build microservices with portability benefits similar to Java EE. We covered in the preceding chapter that the way in which the Java EE standard was developed was making it less suitable for introducing the innovation. How is the MicroProfile different, then?

The microservices scope is not the only essential characteristic of the MicroProfile project. Another characteristic is the way in which the specifications are being developed. Specifications that constitute MicroProfile are developed in a fast, community-based process; if someone has an idea and a need to introduce something to the project, they can propose it to the community (Further reading, link 2). If the idea is accepted, it can be part of the project, released, and presented to the community.

Based on the community feedback, the specification can be amended in the next release. It is crucial to note that the project assumes a fast release cycle as one of its foundations. Taking these two aspects together, we can see why a process is a good tool for introducing innovation: a lightweight community acceptance process, along with a responsive feedback loop, allow for the quick introduction of new ideas and allows them to quickly evolve. This sounds great in theory, but does it work in practice?

The way in which the MicroProfile project gains a momentum seems to confirm that. The initial version of the project consisted only of CDI, JAX-RS, and JSON-P specifications. From that time, as you were able to see in the diagram of the current version, a lot of work has been done and a bunch of new specifications has emerged.

If the new way of developing specifications proves itself, you may be able to avoid the innovation/portability compromise. The rapid evolution of a common specification will allow you to provide innovation at a fast pace, whilst simultaneously keeping the benefits that were the strong points of Java EE: multi-vendor competitive implementation, portability, and interoperability between different implementations.

One more thing to mention is that MicroProfile does not assume that the standardization process is obsolete and that there is no longer a place for it. On the contrary, when one of the MicroProfile specifications reach maturity and proves itself within the community, it will be delegated to a standard body and follow the standardization process.

Jakarta EE

It has been announced that the Java EE brand is changing its name to Jakarta EE, and, similar to MicroProfile, will be a project developed under the governance of the Eclipse foundation. The transformation of the standard is currently taking place, but following the initial success of the MicroProfile initiative it can be expected that the new way in which the standard will be created will learn a lot from its smaller brother, such as the separation of innovation and standardization, and an open community process with fast feedback, providing the latest innovation without sacrificing portability.

If the mentioned efforts prove themselves successful, we can expect a bright future for Enterprise Java being understood as a family of products that originates from the Java EE technology. We will deal with the product based on proven technology, which is based on years of experience and simultaneously alleviating its main drawback by allowing innovation at a fast pace.

Summary

After reading this book, you hopefully have a wider understanding of emerging enterprise software architectures of cloud computing and microservices. Furthermore, you will be familiar with a number of tools that you can use in order to implement systems taking advantage of both of those. We have shown you how to build microservices using WildFly Swarm, and deploy them in the cloud using OpenShift. In the later parts of the book, we have also shown you how to configure Continuous Deployment using Jenkins, security using Keycloak, and how to make your applications resilient to network failures using Hystrix. The emerging solutions of MicroProfile and Jakarta EE will hopefully make it able to innovate enterprise Java in a faster way. As a result, in the near future, you will be able to take advantage of tools that will allow you to solve problems described in this book based on rapidly developed specifications and, as a result, preserve the portability benefits of Java EE.

Further reading

1. `https://microprofile.io/`
2. `https://wiki.eclipse.org/MicroProfile/FeatureInit`
3. `https://projects.eclipse.org/projects/ee4j/charter`

Other Books You May Enjoy

If you enjoyed this book, you may be interested in these other books by Packt:

Mastering Java EE Development with WildFly
Luca Stancapiano

ISBN: 978-1-78728-717-4

- Configure the development environment along with native and cloud installation of WildFly
- Write a DB schema and the relative entities and how to use the relationships between the entities
- Analyze with examples all the java annotations to manage the EJB and the configuration to get better performances
- Write different REST services through the EJB
- Implement Web sockets 1.0 and know why and when use the web sockets
- Work with Active MQ and write JMS clients to manage the authentication and authorization in the clients
- Configure the mail server through the WildFly console
- Learn how and when to use a new feature JAX-RS 2.0, which is the asynchronous call through REST
- Use the new JSF features of Wildfly 10 such as Mojarra 2.2, JSF 2.2, Richfaces 4.5

WildFly Cookbook
Luigi Fugaro

ISBN: 978-1-78439-241-3

- Run WildFly in both standalone and domain operational modes
- Adopt the right profile for your applications
- Configure and manage your WildFly instances with the Admin Console
- Utilize the CLI to deploy, configure, stop, and start service
- Develop HA systems with Apache HTTPD, WildFly, and ModCluster
- Assemble TCP or UDP WildFly clusters
- Deploy your application to the cloud with OpenShift Online
- Use Linux containers with Docker to ship your clean, tested, and ready-to-use WildFly environment

Leave a review - let other readers know what you think

Please share your thoughts on this book with others by leaving a review on the site that you bought it from. If you purchased the book from Amazon, please leave us an honest review on this book's Amazon page. This is vital so that other potential readers can see and use your unbiased opinion to make purchasing decisions, we can understand what our customers think about our products, and our authors can see your feedback on the title that they have worked with Packt to create. It will only take a few minutes of your time, but is valuable to other potential customers, our authors, and Packt. Thank you!

Index

CPSIA information can be obtained
at www.ICGtesting.com
Printed in the USA
LVOW09s0855050418
572195LV00009B/71/P